To. C...

Hap...   1983

Lots of Love DYPS
                        XXX

THE
GOLDEN AGE
OF THE
THAMES

THE
GOLDEN AGE
OF THE
THAMES

Patricia Burstall

DAVID & CHARLES
Newton Abbot   London   North Pomfret (Vt)

Dedicated to the proud and honoured memory
of all those who loved the Thames, but did not
return in 1919 to its brown and placid waters.

Also, with gratitude for patient listening and
'mony lengthen'd sage advices', to one who lives
in spirit in their Golden Age.

British Library Cataloguing in Publication Data
Burstall, Patricia
The golden age of the Thames.
1. Amusements—England—Thames River—History
I. Title
790.1´09422   DA670.T2

ISBN 0–7153–8171–7

Library of Congress Catalog Card Number 80–85496

Filmset in Monophoto Plantin by
Latimer Trend & Company Ltd, Plymouth
and printed in Great Britain
by Biddles Ltd, Guildford, Surrey
for David & Charles (Publishers) Limited
Brunel House   Newton Abbot   Devon

Published in the United States of America
by David & Charles Inc
North Pomfret   Vermont 05053   USA

CONTENTS

THE GOLDEN AGE OF THE THAMES

From about 1870 the Thames above Richmond took on a new character. While flotillas of laden argosies from every quarter of the globe still rounded Kent's tip on course for the Pool of London, higher upstream the river, having ceased to play its historic role as a great commercial highway, became instead perhaps the chief pleasure resort of southern England. A new-found fame brought prosperity to the growing towns and villages of the Thames Valley, especially in the Maidenhead area where for many years the river was presided over by W. H. Turner who kept Boulters lock and by Mr W. H. Grenfell (later Lord Desborough) of Taplow Court. But it was not just the shining gold sovereign which justifies the title of this book. The river in its season was an aristocratic place: the upper classes set the tone, and all other pleasure-seekers, down to the last drunken beanfeaster, were members of a society which, despite individual aberrations, regarded elegance of appearance and dignity of bearing as the norm. Since the Great War dealt England a blow from which she has never recovered, the years before 1914 with their arts and their ideals show ever more clearly as a true golden age, which has drifted from us with the falling leaves of many autumns ever deeper into the gulf of time, to be lost forever.

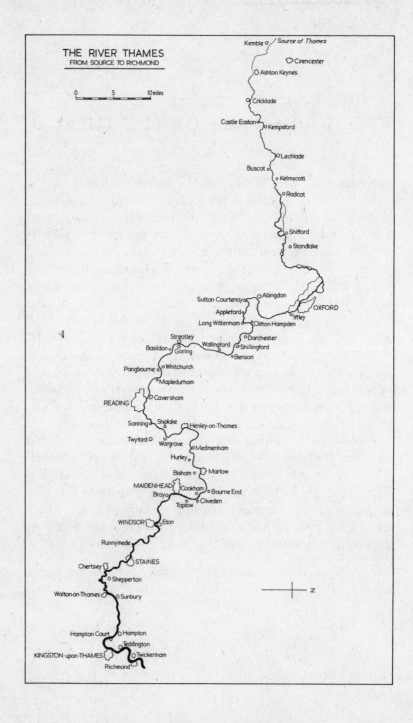

THE RIVER THAMES
FROM SOURCE TO RICHMOND

0   5   10 miles

I

BOULTERS LOCK, ASCOT SUNDAY
1904

In 1904 Turner spent his last Ascot Sunday at Boulters. He is in a sense the hero of this book, for he was a famous man in his day. An ex-naval gunnery and cutlass instructor, 'well-built and muscular, with bronzed face and hands and a sturdy look which fears no man', almost a quarter of a century before he had come to be lock-keeper at Boulters, under the Cliveden woods. There he ruled as the most just and benevolent of dictators—steady, authoritative, courteous, prompt and brave. During his reign he had rescued no less than seven people from drowning, diving into the river with no thought of self, once injuring his arm so badly that for some time afterwards he was unable to use it. His celebrated little lock was wider at the bottom than the top, and it was dangerous to pack vessels tightly together there. Nevertheless, such was his skill that, we are told, he packed boats and launches like barrelled herrings, and his firm commands, sometimes spiced with irony or sarcasm when occasion warranted, enforced obedience. He knew he had to humour the public a little, and that it was no good being angry with them. ' "Now, gentlemen" I say,' he told an interviewer, ' "go quietly", and so they do.'

Anybody who was anybody, and a great many humbler people too, passed through Boulters or joined the lock-loungers there at one time or another, and wherever English was spoken, from the sweltering tropics to the snowy wastes of Canada, from Calcutta to Calgary, there were those who remembered or knew of Turner—Turner and his prize-winning lock garden heavy with the scent of roses, and his sagacious dog Juggins whose knowingness in the matter of biscuits was so remarkable, for he smelt them whenever one of Salter's steamers came into the lock.

Ascot Sunday, which followed the fashionable race meeting, was by 1904 an established function of the social season. As the popularity of the Upper Thames as a pleasure resort had grown, so this event too had grown in importance. The well born, the famous and the merely wealthy flocked to Boulters on that day, models of sartorial elegance, and in their wake others followed, dressed in their smartest, intent to admire and be admired.

On Ascot Sunday 1904 Turner was on duty from 5am until 11pm, and had no time for meals. In the freshness of the summer morning he came out of his rather ugly little greyish-yellow brick house on the lock-side, where the perpetual roaring of Boulters weir made a background to his life. Behind the muslin curtains of luxurious houseboats moored up and down the river, the wealthy and leisured stirred in their sleep as the early light brought to life all the bright colours of the massed flowers which turned their floating homes into miniature gardens. In mansions along the river bank it would be some hours yet before house-party guests descended to their more than lavish breakfasts. But early in the day in many homes in London and in towns and villages within reach of Maidenhead the prettiest costumes and the most becoming hats were donned, the daintiest parasols brought out to set them off and protect delicate complexions, and excited young ladies (perhaps accompanied by stout mammas) and cheerful young men in flannels and striped blazers, with straw hats set at jaunty angles, sallied forth with picnic baskets to railway stations to buy tickets to Maidenhead or Taplow.

Onward flowed the merry crowd. Train doors slammed. Guards pursed their lips and blew sharply on whistles, and engines let forth mighty blasts of steam. Green meadows slid past, and soon came glimpses of the gentle brown river. Then firm masculine hands clasping muslin-clad elbows ensured safe descents on to station platforms. Cabbies, with an avaricious eye to profit, whipped up their horses, hastening to Boulters with a rattle and jingle and clip-clop of trotting hooves, then hurrying back for more fares.

Meanwhile the whirr of the bicycle wheel was heard in

country lane and riverside town, the snorting motor car raised clouds of dust, and horses were harnessed to a variety of vehicles. All these converged on Boulters, and with them a throng of pedestrians. At the fashionable riverside hotels, where mountains of food had been accumulated in readiness, delicious meals were served by hurrying waiters. Boat-builders at Maidenhead, who had greatly expanded their businesses in recent years, hired out their boats and launches.

On that Ascot Sunday, Turner passed 1,000 small craft through Boulters. Some launches were kept waiting for hours, but 182 went through. Many cameras were busy, and the 'cinematograph' also recorded the scene. Never had so many people come to see and be seen, and ropes were placed across the entrance to the lock-side on account of the crowds. Distinguished visitors—including Queen Alexandra—who were staying with Mr Grenfell at Taplow Court on the wooded hill overlooking Boulters, came down to the river to take a trip in an electric launch. The sun sparkled on the glittering waters, and diamond drops rained down from lifted oars. At this most fashionable of locks the ladies appeared in all the glory of the costumes which they had worn at Ascot the previous week, living up to Jerome K. Jerome's dictum: 'Women are the flowers of the earth, and should dress accordingly.' For they made Boulters and its vicinity seem like one huge flowerbed.

It was a romantic age; an age which valued the distinction between the masculine and feminine principles and did not seek to diminish it; an age in which an aura of mystery clung to woman, and in which the fashionable world was a thing to be admired and imitated. By 1904 the highest pinnacle of the arts of civilisation had been reached in England, and although it would be ten years before that civilisation vanished for ever in the great European cataclysm, already the age seemed like a full-blown peony, ripe for falling.

2

THE IRON HORSE

The last chapter showed the Thames at the height of its popularity as a pleasure resort. How did this popularity come about and what enabled it to grow?

In Kensal Green cemetery in West London, amid the crumbling remains of what must surely be the most grandiose collection of tomb architecture ever assembled on English soil to delight the romantic imagination, the observant visitor can find an extremely plain granite slab. It marks the grave of a man who perhaps did more than anyone else to alter the face of Victorian England and, for good or bad, to widen the physical horizons of its ordinary people. He was Isambard Kingdom Brunel, an engineer of genius, who, among other remarkable achievements, was responsible for the planning of the Great Western Railway. Now he lies not far from Paddington station, aptly described as 'Brunel's conservatory', from which the shining rails of 'Brunel's billiard table' (his line to Bristol, so nicknamed on account of the level country through which it runs) pass by the cemetery wall on the first stage of their journey.

Brunel brought the railway to the Thames in the 1830s, and as the years went by branch lines snaked out from his main Bristol line and life at riverside places was deeply affected. Day trippers from London, who would previously never have been seen upstream from Richmond, made a not always welcome appearance in sleepy riparian towns and villages. A more desirable type of summer visitor rented a house for the season, and filled the pockets of local tradesmen. Maidenhead became popular and fashionable. Regattas flourished, professional fishermen earned a living renting their punts and their services by the day to gentlemen anglers, and working class men from London angling clubs had peg-down competitions in the upper reaches. Boat-building firms sprang up and did great business in up-river towns. Hotels were enlarged and modernised, and sometimes fleeced their customers and sometimes had bad seasons but often good ones. Steam launches multiplied, and were loathed by men in small boats. Men in small boats irritated steam launches. Both annoyed anglers. The scene was set for the age of *Three Men in a Boat*.

Hilaire Belloc closes his noble book *The Historic Thames* with a ringing lament for the loss of tradition, and the social revolution, which the Thames Valley suffered on account of the coming of the railway. His concern was with economic organisation and deep underlying historical movements which his special insight enabled him to penetrate. But others regretted in simpler terms the passing of quiet pleasures.

In 1881 the artist G. D. Leslie published a charming book about the Thames entitled *Our River*. He explained in the preface:

> I should not have undertaken such a work, had I not been lately much stirred by feelings of melancholy indignation at the many changes which I have witnessed taking place on the river banks— changes which, though perhaps necessary and unavoidable, are nevertheless slowly but surely destroying the simplicity, the picturesqueness, and the natural beauty so highly prized by artistic river lovers. . . . no doubt in a few years' time a picturesque old wooden weir, with its lashers and bucks, will have become a thing of the past. But there are other changes to be noticed, that have not the plea of necessity in their favour, such as the sewage pollution, the steam-launch nuisance, the erection of ugly bridges and vulgar houses, etc., about which I felt it might not be altogether useless to write in terms of condemnation.

Leslie deplored alterations at Marlow, the destruction of ancient buildings there, and changes at the famous riverside inn, the Compleat Angler, where he had memories of having been served by an old Swiss waiter, Steiner, who spoke broken English and French: 'He is since dead; and on my last visit to the "Angler" I was served by a commonplace London waiter. The little coffee-room, too, had been papered fresh with a modern aesthetic wall-paper—the steady march of culture and taste is so fast and unflinching everywhere.'

Far upstream, at Streatley, a new generation of artists had appeared, of a type and in numbers which called forth Leslie's sarcasm: 'the village swarms with geniuses and their aesthetically dressed wives . . . in the sketching season the little coffee-room at the "Swan" has easels and artists' traps in every corner'. At Maidenhead he saw London pleasure parties at the Orkney Arms Hotel (later always known as Skindles), filling it with their gaiety, show and fashionable slang, and clashing unpleasantly with the gentle dignity of the river. Further downstream, at Staines, Teddington and Kingston, riverside fields suffocated beneath bricks and mortar. The vast development of Maidenhead was yet to come, but huge ugly waterworks offended him at Molesey and Surbiton, gasworks and railway bridges at Staines. Leslie looked back with the sadness of a middle-aged man who remembered the untouched world of his youth.

Population growth contributed to these changes, but even this was chiefly due to the galloping of the iron horse through the quiet pasture lands of the Thames Valley announcing the coming of a new age, of an altogether different world. From the end of the 1830s every shovelful of earth dug from its immemorial resting place and thrown to one side to form part of an embankment soon to be clothed with flowers, trees and grasses; every rock shattered; every sleeper settled in position; and every nail and rivet hammered home, marked one more small step in a process which was to alter beyond recall the towns of the Upper Thames. Over vast areas of the earth's surface the same process was to take place, causing cities to spring up in the wilderness, creating population, trade and prosperity, and destroying in a few decades the silence of the centuries.

3
FROM TREWSBURY MEAD TO TEDDINGTON

The Thames rises in Trewsbury Mead in Gloucestershire, and makes its placid, willow-clad journey eastward across the rich green meadowlands of southern England. The last chapter showed the effect which the building of the railway had on the towns of the upper river in Victorian times. Yet many remote settlements, especially in the highest reaches, escaped its influence. Some were passed by, brooding in deepest countryside. Others indignantly fought off desecration. The Eton College authorities, for instance, were up in arms. They were unable to prevent the railway coming to Windsor, which it reached by branch line in 1849, but their fight kept it from the sacred precincts of college and playing fields. Abingdon and Wallingford also sought to keep intact their ancient peace, but were later reached by branch lines.

In the uppermost reaches the little river flowed between flowery banks, past Kelmscott Manor, the home of William Morris, and on through rich pastures where cows watched with mild curiosity, their muzzles lifted from the sweet-smelling grasses, as a solitary sculler pushed his way amid the tangle of river weeds, passing the innumerable bankside flowers catalogued by Leslie, ranging from frog-bit to lesser scull-cap, from wild strawberries to butter and eggs. Water-lilies flourished in backwaters, growing in undisturbed luxuriance, pink and white like girls' fingers. At Duxford they were found, and, much further downstream, at Laleham by the rushy islets; John Leyland, in *The Thames Illustrated. A Picturesque Journeying from Richmond to Oxford*, noted them also bedecking the stream at Runnymede. Amid the 'inconsolable loneliness' of the stripling Thames, where the air was rich with meadowsweet, bumble bees droned, and a labourer whetted his scythe for the harvest soon to be piled on swaying wains. Far away a dog barked, and a distant stable clock chimed the hour. Birdsong mingled with the river's song, a ceaseless lapping and whispering to itself which it made all the way to the sea. These small sounds blended and became one with the huge silence of the countryside, its chief characteristic.

On flowed the little river, by ancient grey churches, rustic inns, remote locks, and villages with music in the very name of them. Two tributaries, the Windrush and the Evenlode, lovely as their names, came in from the north; then appeared the glories of the great university city of Oxford. Ever wider and a little wider, the Thames passed the ruins of religious houses, once powerful and dominant, small towns in themselves with their clusters of dependent dwellings. Long ago the architectural splendours of Osney Abbey, Abingdon Abbey and, further downstream, Reading and Chertsey Abbeys, had proclaimed them to be among the most important centres of medieval England. A little of Abingdon still remained, but the other three had vanished but for portions of crumbling, ivy-clad walls.

The Sinodun Hills with their traces of ancient for-tifications overlooked the remote and beautiful countryside surrounding Day's lock, and nearby the old town of Dorchester lay dominated by its long grey abbey. Soon, as the Thames flowed on its way, it left behind the honey-coloured stone buildings of the highest reaches, entering a land of mellow red brick and red-tiled roofs. It first encountered the blight of industry at Reading, a town succinctly described by J. Sadler, the lock-keeper at Sonning who was famous in his day for keeping bees and writing verses, as:

> 'mong other things so widely known
> For biscuits, seeds and sauce.

This was soon left behind and Sonning reached—once the seat of a bishopric but now a withdrawn country village, its cottages mantled in roses, jasmine and honeysuckle.

At Henley, a red-brick town dignified by a handsome church and stone bridge, the river put on a new character.

The presiding geniuses of the Golden Age of the Thames:

PLATE 1 Mr W. H. Grenfell (later Lord Desborough) of Taplow Court

PLATE 2 Lock-keeper W. H. Turner of Boulters

Gallant Rowdy.—" There's a selfish chap for you, Jemima; no room for a lady aboard along er him."—
" Where's yer paper collar and yer high glass?"

PLATE 3 'Gallant Rowdy' (*Delightful Thames* by E. D. Manning)

Here it became a place where once a year at the time of the world-famous regatta, high society gathered. Large crowds came to Henley, crowds it is true of the most elegant, superior, strawberries-and-champagne description, but nevertheless crowds who, by their very presence, brought an outside influence to bear on a place which had altered very little through the centuries.

From Marlow downstream the outside influence was felt, becoming ever greater as the river widened Londonwards. Among the many places where riparian development took place was Penton Hook. 'To a select little coterie of people it was *the* place on the river,' wrote G. E. Mitton in *The Thames*, published in 1906. Around this secluded horseshoe of water, bypassed by the main stream, white bungalows sprang up, each with its tiny flower garden from which steps led down to the water. This part was popular with theatrical people, and Ellen Terry had a bungalow there for many years.

An American by the name of Henry Wellington Wack, whose book *In Thamesland* was also published in 1906, was both astonished and scandalised by the sights to be seen in a Teddington backwater. Here many punts were moored and picnics enjoyed beneath the willow trees, and afterwards, before the very wide-open eyes of Mr Wellington Wack:

> Everyone is lying full length in various chamber attitudes, in defiance of all so-called propriety, of every gaze, every expression of wonderment which a foreigner might venture to utter . . . this love dalliance afloat, these lispings and kissings and woodland spooning belong to the swains of Teddington, and no foreigner, habitually living in terror of his own country's police, need waste one gasp in surprise at the sights and sounds, by day or by night, in a Teddington backwater.

4

'THIS WAY TO THE RIVVAH!'

The *Daily Chronicle* reported a familiar London summer scene: ' "This way to the rivvah!" shouted the porters . . . with a mock aristocratic accent that did their sense of humour credit—as the stream of young people in flannels and gay ties and muslin frocks and picture hats made their way up into Paddington.' The *Daily News and Leader* commented on the Sunday morning appearance of that great terminus as:

> . . . extraordinarily lively with bright faces and light dresses—an effervescence of real jollity, and by no means the business-like, Bristol-bound, smoky Paddington of workday unrest and rattle.
> Here the River-Girl (with freckles just beginning to show) presided over the press; porters bowed to her; the station-master, stiff in his silk hat and frock coat, envied her as he waved his Sunday kid gloves for the 'right-away', and wished himself in flannels and a punt; myrmidons staggered in her wake with luncheon-baskets and champagne.

The Golden Age of the Thames was also the golden age of the railway. Money was poured into improving stations and widening the permanent way and poured out again in bigger dividends for the shareholder. Unto him who had it was given. Places which had kept the railway at a distance found themselves becoming backwaters. That was the price they paid for keeping themselves unspotted from the world. But attitudes of the 1840s tended to change later in the century when people had grown more used to noise and disturbance and, having noted the prosperity which these things brought to their neighbours, they sometimes consented to touch pitch to the extent of building branch lines. Places which had poor train services lost business. A. S. Krausse's *A Pictorial History of the River Thames* of 1889 describes how Wallingford, Pangbourne and Sunbury were handicapped in this way.

Walton was little used as a headquarters for boating because the station was over a mile away and the South Western Railway, which served it, had a bad reputation.

Before 1857 Twyford was the station for Henley, the platforms a scene of great bustle and activity on regatta days, and along the intervening road horses' hooves sent up thousands of little puffs of dust. Then the branch line to Henley was opened. G. D. Leslie praised its convenience for the river, saying you could almost step from the station into your boat. Boats could be sent by train, and accompanying crews, provided they numbered not less than four, generally travelled at a reduced fare. Passenger traffic increased by leaps and bounds. 17,696 tickets were bought in 1886; 32,388 in 1895. Between these years six additional sidings were put down in Henley station yard, and the platforms lengthened by 200ft. Before the end of the century the line from Twyford to Henley was doubled in width, and the *Maidenhead Advertiser* commented with satisfaction: 'For this relief we shall surely be thankful. Those stifling crushes, those frantic struggles for a seat, those tedious waitings . . . let them be but faintly recalled in our retrospect of several excursions which began in hope and energy and closed in bitter weariness.'

In 1873 Marlow's little train, the Marlow Donkey, first chuffed its way to Bourne End, which was already connected to Maidenhead and thence to London by the Wycombe branch line. Its passengers looked out on cornfields and pasture and tumuli, the Quarry Woods (which are the 'Wild Wood' of *The Wind in the Willows*), and the green shoulder of Winter Hill. Bourne End banks were bare then, but for the cottage of the ferryman who supplemented his income in wintertime by wood cutting. The Donkey in due course became part of the Great Western Railway system, but in its early days was the shortest independent railway in the world. Passengers steadily increased, and by 1880 the line was becoming profitable to its shareholders. In 1883 there were extra summer trains to and from London. The following year the élite were a little put out at Marlow regatta time when, despite their first-class tickets and fashionable attire, they found themselves sharing a carriage with a rough woman from the harvest fields, carrying a ragged jacket, who appeared very comfortable in her easy seat, and gazed admiringly at the unfamiliar upholstery.

As the 1880s progressed, the station platform was lengthened and edged with Staffordshire bricks. The little railway expanded in all departments, over 3,500 people leaving Marlow by rail after the 1896 regatta; and after that of 1900, three special trains all heavily laden. Not long afterwards Marlow's station master became assistant station master at Paddington which, unless there was some hidden reason for such a fine promotion, must bear witness to the importance of the country line.

The original timber bridge carrying the railway from Cookham to Bourne End on the Wycombe branch line was replaced in the 1890s by a metal construction carried on piles sunk twenty feet into the river bed. Like the Marlow Donkey, trains using this branch line carried their greatest loads at regatta time. Nearly 3,000 travelled by train to Bourne End regatta in 1901.

Maidenhead station was quite inadequate to cope with the vast numbers of people and amount of goods obstructing it during the river season. In the early 1890s the line from Taplow to Twyford was widened, work on Brunel's Sounding Arch over the Thames taking two and a half years. Maidenhead station and its approaches were enlarged then, and stone slabs later replaced the predominantly wooden platform edges. But in 1907 there was still only one window at the booking office, and several years later the *Maidenhead Advertiser* was complaining: 'The narrow stairways giving access to the platforms are continually being blocked by milk churns, laundry hampers, quarters of beef, piano-organs and hat-boxes, which latter have now attained the dimensions of the chaff-basket of the farm-stable.' The booking hall was permanently choked with bicycles, and not until 1913 were arrangements in hand to build a luggage subway with electric lifts and a new parcels office.

This inadequate station dealt with thousands upon thousands of visitors during the season. As early as 1883 there were special trains and extra carriages nearly every Sunday evening. Over two days of Whitsun weekend in 1890, eighteen trains from Paddington ran in duplicate. On Ascot Sunday 1909, four special trains ran to Maidenhead. 2,500 people arrived from London, 500 from Reading, and 500 from Wycombe branch line stations, and on one Sunday night that year 4,000 passengers travelled from or to the station.

One evening proceedings at Maidenhead were enlivened by members of the Metropolitan Minstrel Troupe (mainly Scotland Yard men) returning from a musical river trip. Their train was delayed, and to while away the time they gave an impromptu concert on the station, with a few 'well-executed dances and a little comic business' by a detective. The performance finished with 'Auld Lang Syne', and was much enjoyed by the other waiting passengers.

Many visitors to Boulters lock travelled to Taplow (Maidenhead and Taplow stations being roughly equidistant from Boulters), and in 1896 the platforms there were extended to accommodate them. A reporter from the river magazine the *Lock to Lock Times* was there one Sunday morning a decade earlier, and described the scene as the cheerful crowd waited to hand in their tickets to the 'solitary though good-humoured porter' at the narrow gateway:

> . . . the time taken by this operation gave rise to a good deal of BADINAGE, some of a decidedly personal character. Upon the whole the porter certainly got the best of it, and I have great pleasure in handing his number down to posterity. It was 8,941, and his repeated entreaty to those who were pressing behind to 'take it easy, please, gentlemen', was decidedly mollifying.

The railway attracted passengers by offering cheap excursion tickets to riverside towns. By the 1890s these were introduced for places as far upstream as Wallingford, having already for many years been available to Windsor, Maidenhead, Marlow and Henley. Tickets were offered for combined rail and river trips, and anglers too took advantage of special rates. Members of angling clubs had to show their cards to be eligible to travel to Staines from London for 2s return, to Marlow for 3s 4d or to Goring for 4s 9d.

Excursionists, as later chapters will show, were not always models of decorum, especially when well lubricated with the cup that inebriates as well as cheers. Under the heading 'Ruffianism in Railway Carriages', a passenger who often travelled back to London from Cholsey on Sunday evenings in a train largely patronised by people returning from the river complained to the *Maidenhead Advertiser*:

... a train was delayed for quite fifteen minutes outside Reading, and during the whole of the time a ruffian, hanging half-way out of the window, used the most obscene and blasphemous language possible, at the top of his voice. Surely with a stalwart guard at each end of the train, and with passengers only too ready to identify the man, some steps could be taken.

5
HIGH SOCIETY

One day in June 1896 Turner of Boulters made a lock for one solitary vessel, the steam launch *Duchess*. On board this steamer, beneath a white awning, sat a portly man holding a cigar. A huge, well-behaved crowd packing the river bank and steps of Boulters craned to catch a glimpse of him. Hats were raised and handkerchiefs waved, but the crowd, having regard to the day (which was Sunday), forbore to cheer. The portly man graciously acknowledged the loyal greetings, and the steamer continued on her way.

This large man, irreverently known to his friends as Tum-tum, was a gourmand and a womaniser, whose lack of application and intellect (for his mind rarely rose above the level of the sporting paper the 'Pink 'Un') had many years before been a cause of sorrow to his conscientious parents, Queen Victoria and Prince Albert. Now he was spending Saturday to Monday at Cliveden, the home of the Astors above Boulters, where his fellow-guests included a man of a very different stamp, Lord Roberts VC, a gallant and popular soldier of those golden days of Empire. But Tum-tum—who waited many, many years in the wings before stepping on to the stage as King Edward VII, and during those years attended innumerable race meetings, pursued and captured innumerable ladies, ate an untold number of gigantic meals, and puffed his way through so many cigars that, had they been placed end to end, they would doubtless, like Puck, have put a girdle round the earth—was popular too in his way. A man who devotes his life to the business of enjoying himself, especially if he exhibits in so doing a healthy degree of human weakness, is generally sure of a popularity denied to those who are troubled by the laudable but uncomfortable desire to improve others as well as themselves. Twelve years later, when Tum-tum was King, he gave a huge garden party at Windsor Castle to which were invited representatives of all social classes save the very lowest. Among his guests were Members of Parliament from the infant Labour Party, one of whom, when describing his presentation, exclaimed: 'He is a great King—the people's King. He understands the working classes, and it is no wonder that the working classes love him and would do anything for him.'

The social cachet of Maidenhead, its air of elegance and sophistication as the playground of high society, probably stemmed from the establishment there about 1865 of the Brigade of Guards Boat Club. This in its turn was undoubtedly due to the presence of the railway, and the trains which passed thunderously, emitting vigorous puffs of white smoke, over Brunel's famous brick bridge a little distance downstream, brought immaculate young officers on the quick journey from London. Maidenhead was also within rowing distance of Windsor, which was always garrisoned by the Guards, and within riding distance of Pirbright where battalions were stationed. The Bath road crossed the Thames at Maidenhead by Sir Robert Taylor's handsome eighteenth-century bridge, and thus the boat club was conveniently situated for approach by all means of transport, not forgetting the bicycle. The *Lock to Lock Times* describes an officer of the Household Brigade clad in flannels and with the Guards' ribbon in his hat cycling over the bridge one day in 1888, and makes merry at the expense of a diminutive, sickly looking youth said to have come up to this godlike figure and asked anxiously: 'Do you know that you are wearing the colours of the Lower Tooting Bicycling club?'

Officers of the Brigade of Guards were drawn largely from titled and landed families, and they brought with them to Maidenhead that careless self-confidence sometimes described by the underbred as arrogance, which is natural to those who come from a background of broad acres. Their annual regatta, partly hidden from public gaze by an island parallel to the club, was a grand affair. Guests travelled down to Taplow by special train. They were the cream of society, and 'influential' was the epithet which came most readily to the pen of the reporter on the *Maidenhead Advertiser*. 'Recherché' was the term he applied to the luncheons served to them. Elegant ladies watched the races from the club's lawn. Their gowns, hats (small or shady as fashion dictated) and parasols, and the scarlet uniforms of the band, made a brilliant effect. The Guards regiments took it in turns to supply bands for the regatta, and at the end of each race a few bars of the winner's regimental march were played. Apart from the serious rowing, there were comic events such as mop fights, walking the greasy pole, and dongola races, during which the merry exclamations and laughter wafting from the bank were sometimes blotted out from the competitors as they temporarily disappeared beneath the waters.

Ascot Sunday too was a great occasion at the Guards' boat club. In 1905 over 150 luncheons were served there on that day, and in 1908 a special staff of waiters had to be engaged. The Duchess of Teck was among the guests the following year. Many had tea on the lawn, toying with dainty sandwiches as the sun glinted on the river, and in the flowerbeds geraniums and calcelarias flaunted their bright hues.

At large houses up and down the river, and most notably above the Taplow woods at Taplow Court and Cliveden— those two mansions of contrasting architecture both designed by Sir Charles Barry—house parties were entertained over Ascot week, and at weekends during the river season. Royalty and peers and cabinet ministers, Kitchener whose stern, unflinching gaze was one day to exert a more-than-human power over an entire generation, and the supremely witty Oscar Wilde, repulsive in appearance, 'like a great white slug'—all woke on summer mornings to the sound of birdsong in those woods and, walking beneath the thick-clustered leaves, caught glimpses of the brown waters of Cliveden Reach below.

Householders in riverside towns, and riparian owners, let their homes for the season. Vicars were enabled to take Continental holidays on the proceeds of letting their vicarages. In 1891 the Blue Hungarian Band made music on the lawn of Bray Vicarage, but, as the *Maidenhead Advertiser* hastened to point out, the vicar was not responsible for such frivolity, for a tenant was in residence. In 1912 the Governor of British Columbia rented Bisham Abbey, with its restless ghost, a short way upstream. A wealthy Indian gentleman was at Oakley Court, between Bray and Windsor. Melba used to stay at Maidenhead where she was sometimes seen on the Thames, or near Marlow where her splendid voice, its sound magnified perhaps by the intervening river, could be heard as she practised in her cottage in the Quarry Woods. Actors, actresses and actor managers also favoured Marlow, which was particularly loved by Charles Frohman, the American actor manager, who planned to be buried there and chose the very spot in the churchyard by the river where he wished to lie. But fate had a different end in store for him, for he was to be among the victims of the sinking of the *Lusitania* in 1915.

At Shepperton, at the landing place of the Lincoln Arms, were to be seen about 1890 a mass of boats, most bearing monograms on their sides, sculls and paddles, while on the road above carriages with liveried footmen waited. Lock-loungers at Boulters a few years later watched Mr Sheriff Dewar's announcement of the profitability of the family's whisky trade in the form of three footmen in blue and gold coats, two with powdered hair and the other wearing a white wig, who were in attendance on him and a 'select party' passing through on a launch.

In 1899 Lord Esmé Gordon was staying at Maidenhead where he was chief actor in an undignified scene at Boulters. Trolleys pushed along rails by perspiring men had been installed by the lock to take small craft, thus lessening the queue waiting to go through and speeding the river traffic. Lord Esmé's dog ran over the rails, and a spectator seeing this shouted a warning and the trolley pulled up short. Lord Esmé however, not realising what had happened, and imagining that his dog had been hurt, delivered a tremendous kick on the strategically placed posterior of the stooping trolleyman, accompanying the action with the words, as reported by the *Maidenhead Advertiser*: 'You —— scoundrel to run over my dog!' A policeman employed by the Thames Conservancy who then ordered Lord Esmé off the trolley lines was the next recipient of his wrath, expressed in the terms 'Go to ——!'. He was further informed by the irate nobleman that he would 'knock his —— head off if he interfered with him'. His lordship had not recovered from his chagrin when he visited the lock later in the day and was told that the man he had kicked was laid up, for on receiving this news he exclaimed with satisfaction that he was glad to hear it as his foot had hurt him ever since. The upshot was a court case as a result of which Lord Esmé was fined for assault, obstructing the trolleyway and using obscene language. He also sent his victim £2 to cover his medical expenses and loss of work. The dog, the unwitting cause of this furore, alone remained unscathed, and doubtless continued to crunch bones and sleep curled-up untroubled sleep, after the fashion of his kind.

Any sort of uproar involving anyone with the smallest claim to respectability, let alone a titled person, was rare indeed, although tramps and excursionists and bad lots of various descriptions provided plenty of entertainment for those who found their antics amusing, and caused those who did not to boil with indignation and disgust.

The demands of the fashionable season were imperative. Be the weather never so hot and sunny and the river never so alluring, in the late summer and early autumn the nobility and gentry were no longer to be seen on the Thames. They departed for the seaside, the grouse moors of Scotland and the Swiss mountains, leaving middle and lower class visitors and local people to enjoy the delights of boating and picnicking and launch excursions. Bad weather during the fashionable season could spell disaster for hoteliers, for food had to be laid in whether it was eaten or not, and waiters employed whether they were to be rushed off their feet or left standing like so many gloomy statues, with their napkins over their arms, staring at an endless succession of raindrops travelling down windowpanes, and the chilly, deserted river beyond.

6

LOW SOCIETY

'Our Looker-On', writing in the *Maidenhead Advertiser* of August 1887, devoted himself to a detailed description of that plague of up-river towns, the rough working man on a day's outing who became, as the day wore on, increasingly befuddled with drink. This was the genus known as the beanfeaster, or sometimes as ' 'Arry'. Many came down en masse by train to make excursions in steam launches, and some employed their time drinking themselves silly and then insulting other river-users. The beanfeaster described by 'Our Looker-On', however, arrived in a four-in-hand brake, 'with a battered cornopean braying "Rule Britannia" '. And, the writer goes on:

> Having refreshed himself with a gin-and-bitters, he promenades for half an hour or so outside the hostelry of his choice. He is a scrubby and hairy man, with a limp collar, a rumpled shirt front, and a frock coat disclosing no wristband. He smokes a short clay, and wears his hat on the right side of his head. Another equally familiar type of the genus is a dissipated-looking young man with a red necktie, an aesthetic hat, boots the polishing of which has not been a labour of love, and a meandering watch-guard. There is a big 'feed'—no other word describes the meal—about mid-day, then drinks round, then cigars, then Tommy Dodd for something short, and finally a walk to the river and various aquatic diversions of a grotesque order. Tea in the evening is incomplete without shrimps and salad. Then come more drinks round, Tommy Dodd again, some songs . . . Next a bumper, a few promiscuous twos of gin and whisky, and then heigh for the road again, and 'Auld Lang Syne' on the superannuated cornopean, with 'Britons never, never, never, never shall be slaves' in manly chorus as the suburbs are cleared and familiar objects dance and multiply in an unaccountable way.

'An Old Inhabitant' wrote to the *Maidenhead Advertiser* in 1888 to complain of beanfeasters 'in a beastly state of intoxication' and 'singing and shouting at the tops of their voices, loud enough to be heard a mile away' who had obliged him and several ladies to step off the pavement into the mud to avoid being jostled, if not knocked down. The *Lock to Lock Times* offered ironic advice to 'Arry, suggesting he might quote music hall songs to passing oarsmen, particularly recommending asking 'Does it hurt you much?'; while a bespectacled sculler would be certain to appreciate the greeting, 'Hullo gig-lamps'. Occupants of houseboats, 'Arry was informed, were always grateful for loudly voiced criticism, and enjoyed the spectacle of his beery face staring in at their windows, especially at meal times. The correct approach to a solitary lady occupant was to chaff her, asking 'I say, where's your ma?', to be followed by an enquiry as to when the kettle would be put on. A cartoon in the same journal showed 'Arries and their female companions known as 'Arriets drinking and strumming guitars in a boat called the *Auroarer*.

Sometimes Marlow suffered, as on the July day in the 1880s when a group of 'noisy cads' with linked arms swaggered about in the High Street murdering in cold blood Sankey's 'In the sweet bye and bye'. The absence of the local police at court that day enabled them to give voice unchecked.

The great increase in Sunday river traffic in the 1880s attracted crowds of loafers to Boulters where they earned tips for carrying canoes and other light boats from one side of the lock to the other. In the process they quarrelled with each other, and sometimes with their patrons, and after they had drunk their profits became even more contentious. Bad language invariably followed. One such person was guilty of calling gentlemen '—— toe rags'. The proprietor of Skindles complained that the language of another drunkard had been such that ladies at the hotel had had to close their windows. A stand-up fight one Sunday evening obstructed the road as well as offending the ears of those nearby. Turner had been visited by a deputation who asked him to make what efforts he could to prevent obscene language at the riverside, and he had consequently asked for, and been given, extra police.

In 1892 *The Dwarf*, an illustrated social journal, described

the Sunday scramble at Maidenhead as more than ever like
'the infernal regions': 'Houndsditch was let loose' and
'Petticoat Lane had come out for an airing . . . I expected
some fellows to make a bid for my clothes . . . and I believe to
this moment that my handkerchief remained to me only by a
miracle.' The *Maidenhead Advertiser* not unnaturally took
exception to this view of the mecca of polite society in an age
when the law-abiding majority were protected by an efficient
police force which was in turn backed by stringent criminal
laws, and when the astonishing view that the criminal was
more worthy of pity than his victim would have been laughed
to scorn.

But there was trouble again at Marlow in 1895, when
hobbledehoys removed clothes pegs from a line near the lock
and tried on the clothes, anyone venturing to remonstrate
receiving 'a torrent of genuine Billingsgate'. When walking
through villages they were liable to seize a country girl by the
arm, march her up and down and if possible snatch her hat
and balance it on their own 'beer-fuddled heads', and cottage
gardens might receive their attentions, onions and lettuce
being sampled, and potato haulms pulled up so that they
could see where the potatoes grew. One Saturday in 1896
about 400 rowdy beanfeasters invaded the town, drunkenness
and swearing were rife, and fights broke out.

In 1898 the steam launch *Windsor Castle* entered Cookham
lock bearing disgusting evidence of the bilious state of her
drunken passengers, who entertained themselves by throwing beer, pieces of biscuit and apple and a bit of turf into a
punt drawn up alongside. In Boulters they threw grapeskins
into the lap of a lady in a punt and, when remonstrated with
by her husband, one graciously acknowledged the action,
adding: 'Who the —— are you? Have you bought the river?'
Launch captains were responsible for the good behaviour of
their passengers, and in cases such as this were liable to be
brought up before the courts and fined.

Turner's beautiful garden at Boulters suffered in 1901
when a churlish party on the *River Queen* clambered over an
adjacent launch, landed on the private part of the lock and
damaged his flowers, hooting and yelling at the policeman on

duty as they steamed away. Three years later the *Daily Mail* sent a reporter to Boulters to note the behaviour of launch parties, and he was able to send them an account of a steamer entering the lock towards the end of the day:

> . . . with a third of its occupants—to make a charitable estimate—half drunk; a wretched youth, with the crown torn off his straw hat and cards in his hand, was making mocking bows to some ladies standing at the lock; another man with impudent words offered them cake . . . Big launches are the curse of the river, and drinking is the curse of these big launches; about that everyone is agreed.

The last word in this chapter devoted to him will be left to 'Arry himself, in witty doggerel verses published in the *Lock to Lock Times* in 1888. 'Arry is writing to his friend Bill describing the delights of a launch trip from Molesey. There was:

> Plenty of eatin' and drinkin' on board,
> For the 'eat made us drink, you'll be bound.
> We was moosical too, we'd a cornet,
> Wich Joe 'e blowed 'ard all the time,
> And we sings all the songs as we knows on,
> Oh Crikey! I tell yer t'wos prime . . .
> Hobserved of all the hobservers,
> We made our way quick up the stream,
> For I tell yer a steam-launch can go, wen
> It's properly got up its steam;
> And *larf*, lord I larfed till I busted,
> As we made all the swells scoot away,
> For none of 'em seemed to 'ave trusted,
> Their boats near our launch all the day;
> 'Cept one old galoot who was puntin'
> (That's shovin' a tub with a stick),
> Though 'e tried all 'e knew for to cut it,
> We ran into 'im pooty slick;
> And we yelled as 'e sunk in the river,
> For 'e shouted ' 'elp, 'elp, I'll be drowned',
> 'Ow I wished you were there, t'was a site, Bill,
> I wouldn't a-missed for a pound.
> But 'e managed to get to the shore, then
> 'E sed, sech presumchus darned cheek,
> 'You ought to be 'anged, you are villuns',

And 'e'd ' 'ave us all up 'fore the beak'.
So I ups and I slangs the old buffer,
Well, I thinks as I gave it 'im 'ot,
For 'e walked rite away in disgust, Bill,
As if it was *our* fault, wot rot!
A little while arter, a feller
Arsked if 'e mite 'ang on behind,
So I 'ollers out 'Yus, you are welkum',
For I thort 'ere some sport I should find.
So 'e fastened a rope on to us, Bill
(There was five, two was gells in 'is boat),
We went pooty quick as I told yer,
And 'e 'ardly could keep 'er afloat.
I thort as I'd play 'im a joke, so
I cuts the rope through in a jiff,
And larfter quite made my sides ache as
All at once wrong side up turned the skiff.
And we left 'em a 'owlin' and yellin',
As if they objected to worter;
I do love a joke when it's funny,
And if *you* do not larf, well, you oughter.
'Ere's a yarn, but I've 'eaps more to tell yer,
So expec' soon a letter from me.
We charfed all the swells an' winked at the gells
And 'ad altogether a spree,
We was most of us boozed wen we landed,
And blimy! sech fun you'd ne'er see.
So 'urry up, Bill, get some flannels,
And come up the river with me.
Wen you come bring some 'cham', it's the thing, Bill,
Bring as much as you find you can carry,
Without booze, the river's a fraud, Bill,
So long, no more now from yours, 'Arry.

PLATE 4 Mr W. H. Grenfell, amateur punting champion of the Thames
(*Lock to Lock Times and Flood and Field*, as it was then called, 1891)

PLATE 5 Work on the river bank opposite Medmenham Abbey

PLATE 6 Shooting an old-fashioned weir. The structure of this particular weir was of the movable type, and part of it has been swung away to allow the boat to pass (*Graphic*, 1875)

7

RIPARIAN OWNERS

Were riparian owners red-faced ogres, intent on sealing off backwaters, and driving away from the river flowing by their estates the harmless working man seeking to enjoy with rod and line a few hours' respite from a life of toil? Were they monsters of selfishness, grudging the innocent passing pleasure-seeker so much as a glimpse of their majestic mansions and spacious grounds? Or were they kindly and public-spirited gentlemen who would willingly give those less fortunate than themselves permission to picnic in their woods and camp in their grounds, but were repaid by the destruction of their privacy, the breaking or stealing of their flowers and the use of their trees and shrubs for fuel, and received thanks in the form of deposits of rubbish? The author of *The Royal River*, published in 1885, complained:

> If the holiday-maker is to be traced by scientific investigation, the marks to be looked for will be broken bottles, greasy sandwich-papers, and lobster-shell, just as flint tools and weapons denote other and earlier savages who have lived on the earth, and have made it as disagreeable as possible for their fellow-brutes.

In the middle years of the nineteenth century, riverside houses stood wrapped in a delicious peace. Few sounds broke the repose of their happy owners. The worst they had to fear was an occasional burst of unedifying language from the rough men known as 'scuffle hunters' in attendance on the laden barges which from time to time slid by behind the slow-planted footsteps of straining horses.

But then the changes began in the middle reaches. A. J. Church, writing in *Isis and Thamesis* in the 1880s, sympathised with the riparian owner who wished to keep islands and backwaters private, imagining that he must feel like a dweller in some remote farmhouse which had been

lifted by magic from its rural setting and deposited in
Piccadilly. As always, the majority of pleasure-seekers
behaved well but a minority, the empty spaces in their heads
generally filled with the fumes of alcohol, brought the rest
into disrepute. In place of a few quiet campers, a familiar
sight in the up-river places where they pitched their
inconspicuous tents, came a waterborne invasion at weekends
and holiday times, a spectacle no less fearsome to some local
residents than to the Saxon farmer of the eastern seaboard the
carved prows of approaching Viking longboats rising and
dipping amid the grey wastes of the North Sea. As early as the
1870s began the introduction of 'noisy and questionable
characters' who not only trespassed to picnic but, to the
indignation of a reporter on the *Standard*, impudently
flaunted *chères amies* in their skiffs. Cocky proletarian faces
gaped at ladies and gentlemen enjoying quiet games of
croquet on hitherto secluded riverside lawns. Riparian
properties were treated with a freedom to which roadside
properties were not subject. Music hall songs, not always
melodiously sung, shattered the peace of riparian owners'
nights, and with the invention of the gramophone its strident
tones also came to be heard on the river.

A Mr Tatham who owned islands above Teddington Reach
complained that of the two seats he had placed there one had
been smashed beyond repair and the other chipped. He also
suffered as a result of that desire which especially afflicts the
insignificant and unmemorable to record their presence in a
place, for initials were cut in his expensive camp-shedding.
The *Dictionary of the Thames* published in 1893 by Charles
Dickens, son of the famous novelist, refers to a well-known
camping ground which had been shut by its owner after his
valuable ornamental shrubs had been cut down, his garden
walls climbed, his fruit and eggs stolen and his astonished
cows surreptitiously milked at unholy hours.

Mr Grenfell, one of the most public-spirited men of his
day, referred to the occupants of houseboats and picnickers
in an after-dinner speech in 1884. The former, he
complained, seemed never to go to bed but sang lustily 'to the
accompaniment of a piano very out of tune, or a guitar

confidently played by an amateur' until 2 o'clock in the morning. He never refused picnickers permission to land in his woods, but during the summer he had to employ two men to clear up the rubbish they left behind them.

'Private Water' stated notices. 'Oh, that's all roight', retorted the voices of imperturbable Cockney intruders. 'Come on!' The Thames Rights Defence Association had been formed by 1882 to support members of the public who were 'wrongfully assailed and threatened by riparian owners and occupiers' and battle was joined on the question of riverside proprietors' claims to exclusive fishing rights. The Thames Riparian Owners' Defence Association was formed at the end of 1884 to repel the tide of the vulgar. Before 1885, when legislation made it illegal, shooting had taken place on the river leading to the virtual extermination of the kingfisher there, and placing at hazard of life and limb people in boats, on the towpath, on riverside lawns, and, if we are to believe a member of the Riparian Owners' Defence Association, even within doors. 'Things get unpleasant', he said, 'when they shoot into your dining-room window, break the glasses you have been drinking out of, put a bullet close to your gardener's head, and call him every name they can think of for remonstrating.'

Sir Gilbert East, of Hall Place near Hurley, president of the Association, remembered the old quiet days. In 1861, sculling in his outrigger to Windsor and back, he would pass a good many barges but often no other pleasure-boats. In 1870 he had had one of the first steam launches on the Thames, but by the end of the decade so overwhelmed had the river become with people whom he regarded as little better than savages, that he gave up this vessel. Quite often he had discovered whole boats' crews rolling about among the newly-cut hay of his Hurley farmland, smoking, leaving litter, and cheeking him when rebuked. From the mid 1880s, however, he found an improvement taking place in the general level of behaviour on and by the Thames, the law having stepped in to remind those whom instinct did not of the need to think of the safety and comfort of others as well as their own, and to respect property.

Turner at Boulters lock was also witness to the improved behaviour of river parties, which he too put down to the effect of the new legislation. By the end of the nineteenth century he found little to complain about, except the behaviour of an occasional beanfeast party from London 'who conduct themselves as if the river belonged to them—locks and lock-houses thrown in'. In earlier years he had often seen parties coming down with boughs of lilac, branches of trees and shrubs and handfuls of flowers from riverside gardens, the cause, he said, of grounds being closed to boating parties and camping prohibited.

Readers of *Three Men in a Boat* will remember Jerome's fulminations against riparian owners who sealed off backwaters, but when the evidence is weighed he must be considered biassed (though with the best of comic effect). Riverside residents were also fair game for the *Lock to Lock Times* which in 1888 published a cartoon showing one of them at home with a scarecrow in his garden and surrounded by notices saying 'No Landing', 'Torpedoe [sic] nets can be hired at the next lock', 'Beware of Mine', 'Private Water', 'No Thoroughfare' and 'Beware of Steamroller'. The magazine's Christmas edition that year carried a section headed 'Christmas Eve with Father Thames' in which various types and groups of people associated with the river were featured singing characteristic verses. The riparian owner had a whole arrogant poem to himself beginning:

> I'm monarch of all I survey,
> My right there is none to dispute,
> Least there *is*, but I get my own way,
> Because I'm a selfish old brute.

But the magazine was quick to point out that this attitude was not typical, and gave a list of honourable exceptions.

At Hart's Lock Wood near Goring permission to camp or picnic was freely given by the owner. Milk and hot water were usually available at the keeper's cottage. The owner of Hardwick House Island, upstream from Mapledurham, provided not only a pavilion with table and seats, but also hammocks, a cooking place with fuel, and even baskets of flowers and a visitors' book. Waldorf Astor, who established himself at Cliveden in the 1890s, was clearly of a less trusting disposition. The *Daily Chronicle* reported that the grounds of that mansion were no longer to be open to the public as in the days of its former proprietor, the Duke of Westminster, and that the wooden fences and hedgerows were to be replaced by huge brick walls. 'It looks as if the owner wants to go down to posterity as Mr. "Walled-off" Astor.' But perhaps Mr 'Walled-off' Astor was wise in his generation, for as late as 1907 Sir George Young of Formosa, Cookham, who allowed landing on part of his property, was thanked by having not only his trees and shrubs but also his notice boards and litter boxes used as fuel.

Despite the many discouragements to the generosity of riparian owners, many and many a summer's afternoon saw steamers nudging their slow way to rest by grassy banks and disgorging streams of Sunday school children or London artisans, or stern-eyed temperance groups. Parties were allowed to explore riverside estates, shown round perhaps by dignified head gardeners. Views and flowerbeds and conservatories were admired, cricket played, races run, and tea partaken of under noble trees until the time came for casting off, and then the outlines of steamers, smoke puffing from their funnels, lessened slowly beneath the westering sun. The small notes of piccolos, or the tinkle of pianos accompanied by rollicking baritones or sweet poignant tenors, drew away into the sunset, and when night fell over the land and innumerable tired but happy excursionists laid their heads on pillows in humble bedrooms, exhalations rose from the river meadows wrapping horses and cattle in misty veils, while owls hooted under the harvest moon.

8

THE GRENFELLS OF TAPLOW COURT

The Grenfells of Taplow Court, that romantically turreted red brick mansion above the Taplow Woods, exemplified par excellence the great families of a now vanished England. To wealth, breeding and the habit of command, they added personal distinction, intellectual and athletic achievements and, in the case of Mr Grenfell, tireless public service. Their home was the scene of an endless succession of house parties attended by many of the most famous of the age, from royalty downwards. The enchanting Mrs Grenfell was always surrounded by an admiring group of distinguished men. Mr Grenfell, a remarkable athlete and Amateur Punting Champion of the Upper Thames for a number of years, took the keenest interest in the management of the river and, as Lord Desborough, served for decades as chairman of the Thames Conservancy. Their eldest son Julian, a professional soldier and first rate amateur boxer whose encounters in the ring had marred his good looks (a friend described him as like a Greek statue 'with bits chipped off its face'), was also a poet, whose 'Into Battle' was to become one of the best known poems of the Great War. Their brilliant second son Billy (also a fine boxer) was hoping to become a Fellow of All Souls. These two outstanding young men were to die for their country in the first year of the war, and the only surviving son of the family was to be killed in an accident in the 1920s, but their parents were to live on into the middle years of the twentieth century. What scenes must have come pouring through the floodgates of memory of the aged Lady Desborough as she lay half paralysed in an empty mansion in Hertfordshire, waiting for death with the huge tiredness of old age—scenes of happiness, laughter and companionship, of sadness, desolation and bereavement, of the splendours of life at court, of spring sunshine and primroses in the Taplow Woods.

Every year in November a banquet was held at Taplow Court for the mayor and corporation of Maidenhead and officials of neighbouring boroughs. These gentlemen walked to the dining-room in dignified procession a-glitter with mayoral chains, through the hall which was ornamented with the multitude of medals and silver cups won by Mr Grenfell in various sporting events, and the oars he had used in important rowing races. The dining-room table was sumptuously decorated and softly illuminated by candles massed in a grand candalabrum. The silver shone in their light, which also glinted on more than one occasion on bowls containing young salmon, examples of those which were to stock the Thames, for fishing was among Mr Grenfell's sporting activities on the river. These fish displayed their leaping skill to such effect that some of them had to be retrieved from the table and returned to their bowls by the amused guests.

Another great annual event at Taplow Court, and one in which the whole neighbourhood participated, was the Oddfellows' Fête, which took place in the grounds, and the profits of which were used to pay convalescent home expenses for members of this benevolent society who were recovering from illness. There was all the fun of the fair, with the opportunity to view 'coloured monstrosities' or shy for cigars at the bustle of 'Happy Eliza', to take part in sports, watch stage entertainments, admire the flower gardens and the cedar walk, 'spoon' in secluded nooks, take pony or donkey rides, 'foot it merrily' to the music of a band and, when darkness fell, to gasp with delight at firework snakes and dragons, cheer heartily at the firework thanks to Mr and Mrs Grenfell which always ended the display, and (if one followed the example of a rakish-looking character wearing a deerstalker set at a jaunty angle, who was noticed one year among the last to leave) enliven a somewhat unsteady walk home by singing:

Oh why should we—hic—wait till ter-morrow,
Be—hic—'Queen of my 'art' ter-night.

In 1909 the fête committee and other officials were given a 'sumptuous repast' in the dining-room at Taplow Court. This was the year of Julian Grenfell's twenty-first birthday and he sat at the bottom of the table at which his father (now Lord Desborough) presided. In thanking the Oddfellows for the silver cigarette box presented to him on their behalf by Brother Clout, Julian said that he had tried and always would try to follow in his father's footsteps, 'but', he added drily, 'it is a great shame he has made the pace so hot'.

The Grenfells were descended from a small Cornish squire who founded the family fortunes in the later eighteenth century by starting works at Swansea for smelting copper ores, established himself at Taplow, and became an MP. The parliamentary tradition was followed by subsequent generations, but Lord Desborough was chiefly remarkable for his athletic achievements. As a young man he was simultaneously president of the Oxford University Boat Club and the Athletic Club. He swam the Niagara rapids twice and climbed the Matterhorn three times, sculled a racing skiff across the Channel, and took his Oxford crew in their racing boat over the same route. With two other oarsmen he rowed from Oxford to Putney, overcoming blisters and violent muscular pains and contractions. He was also a British Olympic fencing champion. A magazine reporter sent to Taplow Court to interview him thought it wise to retire to a respectful distance when he tried his strength on the punch ball in the gymnasium in the grounds there. Lord Desborough led an adventurous life and was widely travelled. During the 1880s, while in the Sudan as the *Daily Telegraph*'s war correspondent, he was involved in the affair of General McNeill's zareba, a palisaded enclosure which was being built against the Dervishes. He had just watered his pony Beelzebub. Two sides of the zareba were still unfinished when, 'with fiendish yells the enemy were upon us'. Mules and camels stampeded, Beelzebub disappeared in the bush, panic-stricken hooves churned up clouds of dust so thick that it was impossible to see, and Mr Grenfell (as he was then), armed only with an umbrella, was shot at three times and knocked down six times in the rush, but at last reached Suakim safely. He had visited the Rockies too, spending the daytime hunting, and at night reading all Milton's works including his Latin poems over and over again by the light of a candle stuck in a stick, for, as he said, 'only the best stuff will stand the absolute quiet and stillness of a Rocky Mountain night'. On one occasion he was lost alone in the Bighorn Mountains of Wyoming, watching the moon which seemed to stand still above the canyon in which he wandered in a constant search for wood (for he did not dare to let his fire go out), and from time to time fingering the cartridges in his pocket, which he intended to use if the worst came to the worst.

'In gods and god-like men we put our trust.' Innumerable ordinary mortals put their trust in Mr Grenfell, and he never let them down. He was the champion of river-users and his knowledge of the Thames was so full and detailed that nobody could be of greater use. In later life, after his elevation to the peerage in 1905, it was estimated that he sat on 117 committees. He was captain of Maidenhead Rowing Club and coached its members, and the Oxford crew used to stay at Taplow Court during their training period before the boat race. For a time he was mayor of Maidenhead, and in 1884 was High Steward of the borough, although his duties in the latter capacity were not arduous (they were, as he confessed at a Rowing Club dinner, 'well, none'). He was a great benefactor to the town, and was constantly reaching for his cheque book when donations were needed for local clubs and good causes. He had been instrumental in starting the Thames Punting Club, and his tall, muscular figure was a familiar sight at regattas and punting contests up and down the river where he often acted as judge or umpire, his keen sportsman's eye missing nothing.

Schoolchildren, hundreds at a time (on one occasion as many as 900 from Notting Hill), went on outings to Taplow Court. In 1895, 21 schools had their treats there, a total of 8,000–10,000 children and teachers. In 1893, in the recently built tennis court and gymnasium furnished with tables and seats to accommodate 600 children, members of a Girls' Club were treated to a 'sumptuous tea' at which they were waited on by Mr, Mrs and the Misses Grenfell, some of the gauche young visitors perhaps finding the appearance of their

Herculean host armed with platefuls of buns a rather overwhelming spectacle.

Praise of Mr Grenfell—so active, busy, helpful and successful everywhere from Buckingham Palace to Maidenhead Rowing Club, from India to the Rockies, from the Matterhorn to Maidenhead regatta—was loud and frequent. 'I do not believe', someone wrote of him, 'that in his own chosen way there has ever been a greater Englishman.' A gossip-columnist referred to his 'manly face', his obvious health and strength, and wondered what could induce him to leave the outdoor life for which he was obviously fitted to spend hours a day in the House of Commons and its committee rooms. *Sporting Life* enthused about his athletic appearance, declaring him to have 'the stature, the thews, and sinews of a son of Anak, and the frank free face of one of the Norse sea-kings of years agone', while the *Evening News* pronounced him 'one of the finest men in the House of Commons', telling its readers that:

> . . . his broad, level brow beneath curling light hair, his straight, but not classic nose, his clear, far-seeing eyes, are typically English. His strong neck rises from a pair of broad, supple shoulders, and his arms are as massive as those of some antique hero of the classic sculptures.

To *The World* he was one 'who in his own person represents to an eminent degree those characteristics which have gone to make the supremacy of the race'.

But the last word, restrained but comprehensive, must be left to Turner: ' . . . and then Mr Grenfell, he's got an eye for everything, and he knows what's wanted'.

9

THE THAMES CONSERVANCY

To the Thames Conservancy, which functioned for so many years under Lord Desborough's eagle eye, fell the thankless task of controlling and managing the river.

Although the Thames did not become a famous pleasure resort until two-thirds of the way through Victoria's reign, down through the centuries it had served as a great commercial highway, untroubled by the obstacles which faced travellers by road, but bedevilled by its own problems caused largely by the conflicting interests of millers and barge owners. As commercial traffic had increased, so the charges for the use of locks, towing paths, dams, floodgates 'and other engines' had become exorbitant. (Locks were owned and operated for profit by private individuals until they were taken over by the Thames Conservancy, the name of Day's lock surviving as a reminder of those earlier times.) Parliament intervened in the eighteenth century to check the growing abuses by appointing commissioners to govern the river and settle tolls. But the abuses continued, for the original commissioners had inadequate powers. This led to the appointment of a gigantic new commission later in the century.

The Thames Conservancy was created by an Act of 1857, but for the first nine years of its life controlled only the lower river below Staines. The Thames Navigation Act of 1866 finally abolished the commissioners and placed the entire river under the jurisdiction of the Thames Conservancy. By that time the upper river had fallen into a very poor state. Locks and weirs badly needed attention which the commissioners had been unable to give, having no funds but, on the contrary, a debt of about £88,000 with several years' interest outstanding. The new railway had siphoned off much of their traffic and with it their tolls.

The Port of London Bill of 1908 gave the control of the river below Teddington to the Port of London Authority, and created a new Thames Conservancy to manage the river above that point, whereas the old Conservancy had consisted of two committees whose jurisdiction divided at Staines. Throughout practically all the period covered by this book the upper river was grossly under-represented on the Thames Conservancy. The income of these reaches came partly from tolls (increasingly from pleasure traffic, decreasingly from barges) but mainly from 1878 from payments made by the water companies which filled with Thames water the ewers and bathtubs of London. The Conservancy's finances improved after the passing of the 1911 Thames Conservancy Bill, a new agreement with the Metropolitan Water Board being negotiated.

In a sense it was right that Londoners, daily soaping themselves in their million bathtubs, should through their representatives have a strong voice on the Conservancy Board. The upper river was hampered by poverty, but immediately shied away from any suggestion that the problem could be solved by levying a rate on riparian properties. There were also fears that any increase in London County Council representation on the board would give more support to the water companies at the expense of the upper river, that powers which did not understand rural areas and their hinterland would cause water shortage there by greedy tapping of supplies.

The huge commission appointed in the later eighteenth century, a body so large that, had all its members chosen to meet simultaneously, no hall in existence could have held them, was transformed from a commission into the electorate of the new Thames Conservancy. By the early 1890s suggestions were heard that a substantial number of those still on the electoral roll were in fact inhabitants of churchyards; this however was denied by Sir Gilbert East, who said that in 1889 over 500 names of such sleepers had been removed. At a meeting of the Thames Public Rights Association in 1893, the Thames Conservancy Board was described as 'a curious compound of anomalies and absurdities that was fit to be in the British Museum', the mode of election to which was 'an absolute farce, cumbrous, costly and unsatisfactory in every way'. This system of election was soon to be swept away, not, however, to the satisfaction of Mr J. Bickerdyke, that champion of the common man whose book *Thames Rights and Thames Wrongs* appeared in 1895. Every interest, he declared, was represented on the new board except that of the people of England. Riparian county councils, and the towns of Reading and Oxford, nominated Conservators, and those sitting for the upper river continued to be drawn from the landowning classes. Certainly, no 'Arries were members of the Thames Conservancy!

Among the characters singing in 'Christmas Eve with Father Thames' which featured in the Christmas edition of the *Lock to Lock Times* of 1888 were a chorus of Thames Conservators. 'We haven't got the oof' was the burden of their song. And indeed the lack of an adequate supply of 'oof' or 'tin' with which to pay for the multifarious expenses involved in the management of the river was, it is clear, a constant headache to those dignified, top-hatted gentlemen (although the egalitarian Mr Bickerdyke commented on the fact that, themselves owners of broad acres, they received for their services sums far larger than those needed to cover their expenses). Lock-keepers and other officials had to be paid, locks and weirs renewed, improvements made, pollution controlled, speeding steam launches prosecuted, river law administered, boat races regulated, towing paths maintained, and the river kept navigable by weed-cutting, bush- and tree-lopping, and ceaseless dredging. Dredging was crucial: in dry summers the water level could fall dramatically and in 1884 at low tide cricket was played on the river bed in the channel between the Middlesex shore and Eel Pie Island. Mr Bickerdyke waxed indignant over the Conservancy's failure to maintain the towing path in good condition, which had led to the drowning of some barge horses. He also complained that in some places the Conservancy forbade ferrymen to take anyone not navigating the river. This meant that walkers were excluded, the object being to protect riparian owners' game. The towing path problem was a knotty one, however,

for strictly speaking it was not a footpath, and the Conservancy, which in 1888 owned only a total of 4½ miles of it
between Cricklade and London Stone, had for some years
denied responsibility for making repairs. But a court case
subsequent to the drowning of the barge horses held them
responsible for its upkeep.

The Conservancy was handicapped by having no river
police and no summary jurisdiction. Sometimes a blind eye
had to be turned to infractions of the bye-laws, for the risk of
becoming involved in expensive litigation was too great to be
run. In later, more prosperous years, however, it investigated
complaints about closing of backwaters and tributaries, paid
five officers to travel constantly up and down to check that the
river was open and asked riparian owners, if necessary, to
remove obstructions.

The duties of the Thames Conservancy increased as
subsequent Acts of Parliament tightened its control over the
river. An Act of 1870 enabled it to prevent pollution of
tributaries for a certain distance from their junctions with the
Thames. Another of 1883 sought to check the worst excesses
of those waterborne juggernauts, the steam launches. From
1885, when shooting on and by the river was forbidden, no
longer was it legal for the savagery of man to silence that
delicate musical box within the spotted breast of the thrush,
or destroy the turquoise flashing flight of the kingfisher,
setting it, a small crumpled feathery ball, awash in the
current. Riparian owners, sitting quietly on velvety lawns,
opening *The Times* in the shade of noble trees, were no longer
likely to see before their astonished eyes pellets ripping
through its pristine pages. Their grounds were protected too:
trespassing there, or picking riverside flowers, became criminal offences. Houseboats were not allowed to 'lie or loiter'
where they would. Pleasure boats now had to be registered
with the Thames Conservancy, and steamers carrying over
twelve passengers were to be licensed. Later in the century
pollution was further controlled, the Conservancy being given
powers to prosecute anyone permitting impure matter to
reach the river even from roads. Bylaws were passed to limit
the noise made on the Thames by whistles and sirens: some

steamers, as Mr Grenfell wrote to *The Field*, had sirens more appropriate for Atlantic liners in fog off Newfoundland.

The Thames Conservators had a difficult task to perform. They controlled an upper river suddenly become populous, with the manifold problems this created. They were criticised; they received complaints. They never had enough money. But they did their difficult work to the best of their ability. On taking charge they borrowed a large sum and immediately set about improving locks and weirs. They spent thousands of pounds on the upkeep of the river bank, and in the summer of 1891 were employing 700 men on river conservation. The Conservators themselves made an annual inspection, in their large paddle-boat *Thames*, and as they steamed along—noting that lock-keepers were keeping their locks, that dredgers were dredging, that overhanging trees were being lopped and weeds cleared, and seeing with their own eyes the improvements which had been made in the preceding year—the 'snowy cloth' was laid, and over the brown rippling waters the sound of popping champagne corks was heard. We have it on the evidence of Mr Bickerdyke (he probably disapproved).

10

IMPROVEMENTS ON THE RIVER

Pound locks did not appear on the Thames until the seventeenth century. They replaced weirs composed of frameworks embedded in the river and fitted with 'paddles' of wood placed side by side across their width, which were made to slide up and down in grooves. To enable a boat or barge to travel downstream a few paddles would be raised and the vessel would shoot through on a small rapid. Taking a laden barge upstream before the days of pound locks was a difficult and dangerous process. All the paddles would be drawn up creating a 'flash', and against the water rushing down in a lively but wide current the barge would be hauled up by winches, capstans, horses, or gangs of as many as eighty men.

Pound locks existed at Iffley, Sandford and Swift Ditch by 1635, but elsewhere the awkward and unsatisfactory old-fashioned system impeded traffic until the coming of the canal age brought a new outlook. Then they began to be built in far greater numbers, and by 1810 there were twenty-seven of them. The canal reaching Oxford from Birmingham in 1790 gave the impetus for the construction of modern locks on the Thames there.

If the railway created the Golden Age of the Thames, these locks made it possible and gave it its character and focal points. But Walter Higgins, in his book *Father Thames*, lamented the passing of the earlier structures which had 'gone the way of all ancient and delightful things, and in their place we have the thoroughly effective "pound-locks" . . . which in reality convert the river into a long series of water-terraces or steps, dropping lower and lower the nearer we approach the mouth'. By late Victorian times the locks of the canal age had settled out of true and become, in their turn, picturesque, old-fashioned and lovable. They were unable to cope with the traffic then thrust upon them, becoming expensive headaches

PLATE 7 'Summer Life on the Thames: A Luncheon Party on a Houseboat at Henley' (*The Black & White Magazine*, 1880s)

PLATE 8 'Squash', a negro minstrel who was well-known at Henley (*Illustrated London News*)

PLATE 9 The most elegant form of transport outside the most elegant riverside hotel

PLATE 10 A popular form of transport to the river

for the officials of the Thames Conservancy. In H. R. Robertson's *Life on the Upper Thames*, published in 1875 just as the upper river was entering into the age of its great popularity as a pleasure resort, we read a lament for the new become old:

> ... the quaint old constructions of irregular wood-work ... are gradually making way for successors of 'improved' modern style. With side-walls of square blocks of concrete, and smooth gates as black as pitch can make them, they lose all charm of appearance. The action, too, of opening the gates by leaning the back against the swing-beam ... is fast becoming obsolete, giving way to a mechanical apparatus with wheel and axle.

From the 1870s onwards the Thames Conservancy regularly rebuilt or improved their locks and weirs, often enlarging and sometimes resiting them. Benson, Cleeve and Whitchurch, and Caversham locks were dealt with in the 1870s; Hambledon, Bray and Old Windsor in the 1880s; Temple, Rushey and Boveney in the 1890s; Sonning, Shepperton, Molesey, Mapledurham and Penton Hook in the 1900s; and Boulters, the most famous of all, in 1912. Teddington lock-cut was widened, because of the great increase in pleasure traffic, in 1890, and in 1904 a mammoth lock was built there to cope with the tidal barge traffic. A half-tide lock was built at Richmond in 1894.

Trolleys to enable small craft to bypass the queue for the lock were installed at Temple and Boveney as well as at Boulters. As the great entertainment at Boulters was to see and be seen, this excellent system did not meet with the popularity which it deserved with boating people there. On account of the trolleys' great weight, their iron buffers, and the worn state of the shingle path, pushing them was exhausting work for the trolley men who were sometimes knocked up by the heat and labour, and on at least one occasion the rollers had to be stopped for a time to enable them to rest. A letter to the *Lock to Lock Times* in 1893 complained of the 'cumbersome, broken-down' old roller at Boulters. When Turner first became lock-keeper there the lock-side had been a grassy bank, but by the end of the nineteenth century the Thames Conservancy had spent well over £1,000 on improvements, so that in addition to the trolley and boat slips, there was a landing place for launch parties, an 'artistic' shelter where the lock assistants could munch their 'thumb-bits', which they formerly had to eat in full view of the public, an improved apparatus for raising the sluices and steps to replace the grassy bank. In 1896 a double line of metals was laid forming a railway on which the trolleys could be pushed, taking twice as many boats again as the old rollers. This new system worked splendidly, and the men in charge were able to take little rides when the trolleys returned empty.

In 1899 a furore was caused by the fencing in of Boulters. 'Fancy Brighton Corporation railing off part of the sea-front because the crowd on the shingle impeded the launching and beaching of boats or disturbed the bathers!' commented the *Paddington Times*. Apparently the less desirable class among the lock-loungers had made a nuisance of itself, and from the perspiring faces of dusty, begrimed cyclists had issued rude remarks offensive to the elegantly attired ladies and gentlemen passing through the lock. 'Boulters lock in a cage and Turner like a performing—no! I cannot write that word!' exclaimed 'Our Looker-On' in the *Maidenhead Advertiser*. A footpaths society was preparing to take action against the Thames Conservancy for blocking the path, and Maidenhead Town Council threatened to take legal action if the Conservancy failed to remove the fence within seven days. The storm soon blew over, and the closing of his lock-side was left to Turner's discretion; in practice he nearly always allowed it to remain open to the public.

When the lock was enlarged in 1912 the trolley road was in its turn replaced by a mechanical boat elevator operating on the same principle as 'the revolving staircases now so popular in the chief business establishments of London', or the 'Jack-ladder' of Canadian lumber mills. It attracted about 1,300 boats the first Sunday after it was opened in 1913, the novelty of the ride doubtless compensating for its speed.

The new Boulters lock was longer, wider and straighter than the old, the walls of which had become eight inches out of true. While alterations were in progress, an estimated thirteen million gallons of water were pumped away daily, the whole bottom of the excavation being virtually one large spring. The famous old flour mill on Ray Mill Island had to be demolished, and the pretty little bridge leading to it was replaced by a larger one. The lock gates were to be manipulated by quadrants and winches to give J. Harrison (Turner's successor) and his assistants a less 'perspiring time' of it on busy days. A large crowd assembled for the reopening ceremony, and Lord Desborough, wielding a silver trowel with ivory handle, laid the commemorative stone in his usual workmanlike fashion.

The *Daily Telegraph* reporter was saddened by the loss of picturesqueness caused by the improvements at Boulters. The romantic old water gate and the ancient steps were gone, ironwork and iron railing replaced mellowed and moss-grown timber. The *Standard* reporter described the boat elevator as very efficient, but said it banished 'that beautiful mass of tints from gay parasols and multi-coloured blazers, which filled the lock in the days before progress came along'. The Boulters of Ascot Sunday he called the Charing Cross of the Thames, but since the alterations it 'seemed to have lost a good deal of its old-time grace and animation. The boat-men readily confirmed this; indeed, one went so far as to say that the day of Boulters lock was over.'

But then the whole world of Boulters was over. The year was 1914.

11

HENLEY REGATTA

The glory of Boulters lasted throughout the fashionable river season. Henley's hour was shorter, but not less glorious, for its regatta had become 'the greatest aquatic carnival of Christendom'.

A very old man died as 1910 made its chill entry into the procession of the years. He was born before Waterloo, almost outlived Edward VII, and as a youth had been an eye-witness of the first university boat race, which took place at Henley in 1829. That was long before the days of sliding seats, and a rowing man's success depended then on the strength of his arms. A huge crowd of supporters had driven over from Oxford in a variety of smart vehicles behind some unexceptionable horseflesh. Their crew were dressed in blue checks; Cambridge, who rowed a heavy tub, were clad in white with pink waistbands (the Cambridge favours were then pink). When Oxford won, a shout rose over the grey stone bridge and church and the mellow brickwork and old red tiles of the little town such as had probably never been heard there before. It lost itself amid the hills, which gave back its echo.

This was the first great rowing event at Henley. Over the next ten years various contests took place over the same course. Regattas were being started all over the country, and in 1839 funds were collected and the Grand Challenge Cup was first competed for. Henley regatta was born. The cup was an ornate affair, its handles ornamented with masks and plants, water plants growing up its stem to a pattern of waves, and above them the recumbent figure of Father Thames clad only in a luxuriant beard. It cost 100 guineas—a great deal of money in those days.

Rowing gradually established itself as a respectable sport at the public schools and universities. The Oxford University

Boat Club was founded in the same year as Henley regatta, but it was some time before official blessing was given to its members competing there. Even in 1851, despite the fact that in that year the immaculate Prince Albert honoured the event with his patronage, Oxford college crews were entering under false names. The presence and identity of the members of a crew from Christ Church was let slip by a newspaper reporter with the result that the offending undergraduates were rusticated for a term. The Eton Eight was first seen at Henley in 1854, but did not actually take part in the regatta until 1861. Not long before Mr (later Dr) E. Warre, a former pupil and future headmaster, a rowing man and member of the Leander Club, had returned as a master to his old school, and was to be seen of an evening along the towpath coaching its eight. Radley also competed at Henley in 1861, and two years later so numerous were the entries that it was suggested that the regatta be extended to three days. The opening of the railway station in the 1850s enabled a much wider public to attend the regatta. Over the years a greater range of public schools came to take part; and the first overseas competitor (from America) appeared in 1872.

Why should regattas held at Henley, a quiet country place on a branch line, have become world-famous events, imperatives of the fashionable season, whereas Maidenhead—a rapidly developing town on the main line, much more conveniently placed for London and Windsor, the home of the Brigade of Guards Boat Club and Boulters lock—failed to compete, and indeed for a long time held its regattas jointly with Marlow (in fact for five or six years in the 1870s in Marlow's Reach)? A curious failure, it might seem, for a town which developed into the mecca of polite society throughout the appropriate weeks each summer, and on Ascot Sunday boasted in its immediate vicinity an amount of blue blood equal in quantity to all the alcoholic beverages required to make every 'Arry see double and sing off key for all the rest of the year!

It was impossible to make Henley's course completely fair, although the competitors' chances became more equal after 1885 when it was altered to start further downstream with the finishing post at Poplar Point, about four hundred yards below the bridge where the river makes a sudden bend to the east which, unless a cross wind from the west favoured the crew on the Buckinghamshire shore, had previously given a decisive advantage to their rivals. But it is a wide course, unimpeded by eyots and superior to Maidenhead's, its open position giving spectators a fine, clear view. Maidenhead suffered too from the 'old and insuperable difficulty of carriage accommodation'. The selection of Henley for the first university boat race, and the attraction of its regatta to university and public school crews, set the seal of fashionable approval on it. Such crews and their supporters were not dependent on the railway for transport, nor was the greater accessibility of Maidenhead from London important to them. The Brigade of Guards Boat Club did indeed hold its regatta at Maidenhead each year, but that very exclusive event was of a semi-private character, and beyond the fact that they contributed to the funds of the local regatta the presence of the Guards' clubhouse had no effect on it. And so it came about that these two up-river towns divided between them the éclat (and the profits) of the fashionable river season in this particular way.

The effects of Henley regatta were felt far and wide, up and down stream. For every competitor, for every spectator, there were others to supply their needs, providing food, shelter, clothing and entertainment—champagne, strawberries and cigars, hotels and houseboats, straw hats and parasols, banjos, pianos and fireworks—many of whom would never in their lives watch the sun's golden pathway on Thames waters. Dressmakers sewing with small neat stitches, ladies' maids taking rustling gowns from mahogany wardrobes, valets stropping razors, and boot boys polishing boots all made their contribution. Lobsters crawling along the briny seabed, grapes ripening in Burgundian vineyards, chickens pecking in distant farmyards, silkworms devouring mulberry leaves, and ostriches bearing fine tufts of feathers on their unsuspecting posteriors, all sooner or later played their part.

As the time of the great regatta approached, rooms were swept and garnished, curtains washed, beds made up, supplies of food laid in and apartments let, not only in Henley itself where costs were often very high, but in the surrounding district, at Marlow for instance. Local tradesmen, according to their wares, were gratified if unexpected downpours caused a rush for mackintoshes and umbrellas, or hoped that a heat wave would cause perspiration to remove the starch from swells' shirt fronts and necessitate further purchases for evening parties. Houseboats moved to take up their positions along the bank and, by 1909 if not before, a large-scale map at the Thames Conservancy office showed the position of every one which had applied for a place, drawings to scale being cut out and pasted on. Local nurserymen did a flourishing trade and untold thousands of flowers and plants decorating houseboats turned the river's edge into one huge floating garden. Boats were hired in advance up and down stream. In 1890 Tagg's of Hampton Court erected a large landing stage at Henley, and offered a wide selection there. Private boats, loaded on carts, approached the town from all directions, and neighbouring lock-keepers slaved early and late, both before and after the regatta.

Cockneys, their faces blackened with burnt cork, were transformed into negro minstrels. According to the *Maidenhead Advertiser* in 1887, a troupe of them:

> . . . went up to the Royal launch . . . and commenced their minstrelsy. An official would have ordered their immediate removal, but observing that the Royal party seemed to enjoy the comicalities of the darkies, and receiving no indication that they were regarded as objectionable, he allowed them to remain. The Prince and his party contributed liberally to the serenaders' net.

But things were not always so good, it seems, for in 1891 a minstrel took into his confidence a cleric by whom he chanced to sit in the train down from Paddington. For twenty-five years, he said, he had been going to Henley. But 'niggering', he complained, was not what it used to be.

High and low were catered for, and money made in all sorts of ways, from the sale of whelks or 'penny ticklers' to the efforts of the man who let you tie him up with a clothes line and then untied himself. Thieves and pickpockets regarded the regatta with interest, but their optimism was less well founded from 1894 onwards when a new road was made for vehicles and there were no longer crushes of pedestrians at the old steps. And the police were always watchful.

Rowing men stayed at the Red Lion. From the street you could see their clean-cut profiles at upstairs windows or watch their faces looking out on the busy scene as they appraised the boats passing by road or already afloat, surveyed the river and discussed their prospects. Or you found them, clad in flannels, blazers and straw hats, leaning against the parapet of the bridge or sitting on it swinging their legs, yarning about old triumphs or defeats.

In the early days of the regatta the gentry watched from their carriages on the bridge and lesser people stood on the banks, but as the years went by it became the custom to survey the scene from boats packed so tightly together that you could walk from one to another half way across the river. Controlling this mass of boats so as to keep the course clear for the races was a problem for the officials. By 1894 fewer apartments were taken for the regatta as the railway made day trips so easy. The previous year 26,809 people had travelled down by train for the occasion.

Houseboats—floating palaces sparkling with fairy lights by night, luxuriously furnished, and inhabited by remote romantic figures from the world of high society and high fashion—were perhaps the greatest attractions to the general public at regatta time. But they too brought problems in their train. Before the Thames Conservancy took matters in hand in 1888, there was a great scramble for places. After the Conservancy introduced a system of allocation, speculators applied early, made sure that their houseboats were placed in the best positions, and then tried to let them for exorbitant sums, leaving genuine owners to be placed far down the reach, although in theory those subscribing to the regatta funds, and living regularly on their own boats, should have been given the favoured positions. An edict tried to prevent houseboats being turned into 'floating hotels'. In 1889 there were 150 at Henley, but by the end of the century their numbers, though not their brilliance, were in decline. The new rules introduced by the Thames Conservancy reduced them to about sixty in 1898, and local people who let their houses at huge profits for the regatta period, to those whom houseboat owners brought down with them, complained bitterly.

As the heyday of the houseboat passed at Henley, club enclosures became more popular. In 1909 the public could buy tickets for Phyllis Court Club visitors' enclosure at 15s 6d for one day or £1 17s 6d for the three. We often hear of Phyllis Court in the early years of the century, of ladies wearing 'choicest confections' gathered in little groups on its lawn; of its appearance at night, as a 'veritable fairyland' of lights; of the ballet *Heartsease* given there with a chorus of 200 and orchestra from London augmented by a military band. The Bath and the Sports Clubs were crowded with members and guests at regatta times, as were the Leander, Grosvenor, New Oxford and Cambridge. Lesser mortals camped on Parrott's Island.

G. D. Leslie describes a terrible crush at Marsh lock just upstream from Henley on regatta morning. The mass of boats formed a huge arrowhead, tightening up when the gates opened, each eager to get in first (especially the ladies!). As the lock filled the boats jammed together, the sides of some giving way with ominous creaks. Outriggers and rowlocks were crushed and broken, there were cries and abuse, the excitement mounted, the regatta gun could be heard signalling the start of the first race, 'and the instant the lower gates could be opened the whole crowd of boats rushed out, splash, dash, and away, like school boys out of school'.

People went to Henley for many different reasons, among which an interest in the manly efforts and good-natured sportsmanship of the competitors was not always paramount. There was no doubt, however, in the case of the vicar of Hurley, who in 1894 was seen rushing along the river bank with a crowd of shouting supporters. Clerical dignity was forgotten, and far from his mind was the Holy Sacrament and the laying on of hands. His years fell from him. The bottoms of his trousers were stuffed into the tops of his socks and he flew along the towpath, roaring himself hoarse, imploring Radley to win.

12

OTHER REGATTAS AND THE 'AMATEUR' QUESTION

As the luxuriant richness of high summer settled over the Thames Valley countryside and the early, then the late, harvest bent gold to the reaper's scythe; as cattle clustered in ponds or in the shade of trees vainly seeking relief from the tormenting flies encrusting their eyes; as cats dozed in farmyards yawning from time to time to show the pink insides of their mouths and their rows of wicked little teeth, so up and down the river bank the human inhabitants of that favoured valley gathered to enjoy their regatta times. Some regattas were old-established but had lapsed and were revived, as that of Richmond and Twickenham which was re-established in 1890 after an interval of forty years; others, such as that of Bourne End, were held for the first time as little communities on the river bank grew to a reasonable size.

Many an anxious glance was cast skywards as these galas approached, and amateur weather prophets read the signs of the heavens. Sometimes oarsmen struggled against blustery north-east winds, ladies wore their furs, and the only warmth, as the *Maidenhead Advertiser* was known to observe, was created by the language of cabbies which, on account of the paucity of their business, was of a somewhat 'burning' description. Sometimes rain made oarsmen's blades slippery as if they had been coated with grease, and fell in drops from the nose-ends of those unlucky contestants; ladies wore oilskins over their pretty costumes, and large hats were never taken from their boxes. But often 'Old Sol' was gracious and then a kaleidoscopic effect obtained along the river bank, made up of gowns and gloves and ribbons, hats and parasols and blazers, the red uniforms of the military bands, the awnings, flowers and paintwork of houseboats and launches. Sometimes indeed the heat was almost tropical and spectators watched from the shelter of trees while the oarsmen toiled along in the full glare of the sun, its brightness reflected back into their eyes by the thousand winking ripples of the river's surface.

'Regatta' is a Venetian term, and its earliest known use in England was in 1775 when it was applied to a water pageant held on the Thames at London. Rowing was not, of course, in earlier centuries regarded as an occupation suitable for gentlemen. Watermen were hired to row customers to their destinations by river, as coachmen were employed to drive them by land. But just as Regency bucks enjoyed taking the reins and bowling along the dusty roads showing their own skill and their horses' speed, so rowing (although working men continued to make their living by it, and Eton heads had earlier regarded it as 'a low pursuit') came to be seen as a challenging sport for young sprigs of the gentry and aristocracy. Mr Grenfell pointed out the moral benefits to be gained from the self-sacrifice, self-effacement and team work it necessitated, holding that more was to be learnt from the field of athletics than from books.

Even after rowing was established as a sport for amateurs, done purely for its own sake as an exercise and trial of skill, its professional connections lingered; the distinction between 'amateur' and 'professional', dating from before the days of the great popularity of rowing, was still governing competitions at the end of the century. An amateur, as defined at a meeting of the stewards and committee of Henley regatta in 1879, must never have competed in any open competition for money, or against a professional for any prize, have taught or pursued athletic exercises of any kind for a living, have been employed with boats for money, be employed or have been employed for wages or be a mechanic, artisan or labourer. Mr Grenfell was anxious to exclude foreign entries from Henley for a variety of reasons, and Dr Warre of Eton felt that abroad, especially in America, too much of a profession was made of training for athletic competitions.

The rules regarding amateurs came to handicap rowing club officials making up regatta crews as best they might of pale clerks and grocers, while marking with covetous eyes the muscular development of passing roadsweepers. They also led to anomalies, as that which entitled the smallest shop-keeper to enter the charmed circle, but excluded, for instance, a silversmith. In the 1890s, 'Trifler' of the *Maidenhead Advertiser* was indignant that the Amateur Rowing Association, which he described as 'this body of wiseacres', had:

> . . . positively declined to alter the absurd and inconsistent rule defining an *amateur*—a rule that must have been framed by a clique of kid-gloved and top-hatted but small-brained and conceited aristocrats, who have seen little of the world outside the walls of Oxford or Cambridge colleges.

But a letter to the *Lock to Lock Times* put another point of view. Why go out of the way to promote discord? asked the writer, observing that people liked to associate with those of their own rank. Ladies, too, were taken to the clubhouse, and much of the pleasure of club life would vanish if bricklayers and bargees 'could air their unstudied language and unceremonious manners' there.

But regattas for all types and conditions of men took place up and down the river, and at one or the other all had a chance to show their skill with blade or punt-pole, or struggle along a greasy pole suspended over the river and try to reach and seize the joint of meat suspended at its end, no matter how unstudied their language (which it doubtless was when they fell in). Towns held their yearly regattas, and at Henley, for instance, there were two—the famous society function, and a much smaller local one later in the season. In 1890 and 1891 the *Lock to Lock Times* made reference to regattas for Maidenhead Watermen, Wargrave and Reading Working Men, the Royal Engineering College at Coopers Hill (to be held at Windsor), the Second Life Guards (at Datchet) and the towns or villages of Henley, Marlow, Reading, Cookham, Goring and Streatley, Wargrave and Molesey. Amateur fours from Goring—Manor Cottage Crew, Glebe Cottage Four, the Vicarage crew—tell by their very names of a rustic England now lost in the mists of time, of an ordered society, of sedate village church-going, of matins and evensong and saints' days, and of hymns and psalms and responses drifting out from musty church interiors on the sweet air of summer Sundays.

Regattas held for watermen and fishermen had a charitable purpose. Money prizes helped to keep their winners through the lean days of winter, while the fat goose prize hanging in a basket at the end of a greasy pole at the Henley Watermen's regatta of 1884, and the pig competed for at Marlow in 1890, must have brought exclamations of delight when they arrived at cottage doorways—the pig probably protesting loudly—and wives and families crowded to see, asking themselves (in rather different words of course):

What conquest brings he home?
What tributaries follow him to Rome
To grace in captive bonds his chariot wheels?

Members of the Riverside Club at Maidenhead, which was established for a time in buildings later taken over by the Brigade of Guards when the latter left their smaller premises now part of Skindles, contributed funds to enable a regatta to be held for their servants. A band played, and club members watched and applauded from their lawn, while their eyot was used as an enclosure for the competitors' friends.

Benefactions were many. As was to be expected, Mr Grenfell was to the fore, donating a silver goblet for the Windsor and Eton regatta in 1891, and a cup for the Single Punting Handicap there some years later. Prominent people up and down the river, such as Mr G. Palmer of the Reading biscuit firm and Mr M. Sutton Jnr of the seed firm, gave challenge cups and prizes. Mrs Annie Smith, who lived at 'The Fishery' (later renamed Farnah House) near Maidenhead bridge, was especially generous and, as well as giving money and prizes to local regattas, organised punting races for her own servants in 1892, after which she 'generously regaled the competitors and distributed the prizes'. On another occasion she gave a day of aquatic sports and pastimes, providing prizes, band, refreshments for the competitors, tea for her many guests, and fireworks which went off prematurely causing a hasty scattering of nearby spectators. A telegram was sent for a further supply of fireworks, and the sonorous tones of the town crier announced this fact to the assembled company.

Lawns and launches were lent by the wealthy for the use of regatta committees and rowing club members; and the King of Siam who was staying at Taplow Court in the summer of 1897 responded to a hint dropped by the referee of the Maidenhead Engineers' and Fishermen's regatta, giving as prize a solid silver bowl in the shape of a huge open lily. He was probably repaid by the amusement given to the crown prince who watched the rowing and the greasy pole contest. Messrs Lever Brothers were clearly determined not to be outdone by the generosity of others, for they gave cups as prizes for sculling contests, accompanied by boxes of Sunlight soap, which served the dual purpose of advertising their wares and ensuring that winners did not go dirty.

Regatta funds were supplemented as the years went on by the increasing use of the flag scheme whereby boats and launches contributed half-a-crown apiece. House to house collections were also made in advance and collectors normally did well. In 1901 for instance, about £100 and some prizes were given by local residents for the Maidenhead Engineers' and Fishermen's regatta.

Cookham regatta was often blessed with good weather. It was estimated that nearly 10,000 people attended in 1890, when scarlet drapery on the bandstand in Bell Rope meadow matched the uniforms of the band of the Grenadier Guards, dazzlingly bright in the sunshine. Steam launches were decorated with wild flowers from nearby meadows, among which predominated crimson poppies come crumpled into the world from their tight green packing cases, innocent then of the bitter symbolism they were to carry for later generations. The houseboat *Siesta* was ornamented by a huge Japanese fan on either end, while the *Golden Grasshopper* had painted sabots as flower-holders. There were six other houseboats, and 'the graceful Venetian gondola from Abney House was also to be seen now and again, manipulated by its native gondolier'. The racing was close and interesting, with the exception of the amateur punting, for Mr Grenfell was competing, and left his rivals far behind. Punting was an important feature of this regatta. In 1891 the Cookham lock-keeper, A. Hill, and his partner won the double race for local watermen which was incorporated into the day's events, and a few years later the ladies' punting competition lasted no less than four hours, one lady scoring full marks. Meanwhile 'a few itinerant musicians sang comic ditties to banjo accompaniment, encouraged by contributions in bronze from a suffering public'.

Comic balloons sometimes featured at Cookham regatta. One year an elephant balloon was reluctant to ascend. On being kicked, he knocked a hedge, turned to scowl, and finally roosted on the top of a high elm. No such inhibition, however, had affected a representation of Mr Gladstone, that peculiarly Victorian figure, who, with arms outstretched in benediction over the laughing faces below, sailed serenely away into the bright August sunshine of 1888.

13

VENETIAN FÊTES AND RIVER CONCERTS

From Bisham churchyard path the river comes in view, its shining grey surface seen between gravestones, their outlines softened by the boughs of a pendent ash. Near the church door in a grave marked by a stone cross carved to represent rough-barked wood, now mossy with the lapse of years, lies Charles M. Foottit, once proprietor of the Compleat Angler by Marlow bridge, who died at an early age in 1896.

The Anglers, as it was called, had been in Mr Foottit's family for a century, and he himself was described by the *Lock to Lock Times* as an institution in Marlow, one of the most sociable men on the river bank, giving the impression of being 'a right down good fellow'. He was responsible for bringing from Venice to the Thames what must surely have been the prettiest custom ever seen between its gentle banks—that of the Venetian fête.

The earliest record of a procession of illuminated boats is at Marlow after the town regatta in 1884; and such fêtes, accompanied by firework displays and the brilliant illumination of riverside houses and houseboats, became customary finales to regatta days up and down the Thames. Concerts on and by the water, too, both expressed and added to the beauty of those magical evenings. At Marlow in 1884 the procession consisted of about fifty boats, their Chinese lanterns and coloured lights reflected waveringly in the black river, 'the whole presenting a fairy-like and brilliant appearance'. By the following summer the number of boats taking part had grown to nearly 150. The town band played as they floated down from Bisham church past brightly lit buildings and lawns, and because even in fairyland there is profit to be made, Mr Toovey who supplied the lights did brisk business.

By 1887 Mr Foottit's houseboat the *Evelyn* was leading the

PLATE 11 The wealthy classes succumbed en masse to the motoring craze, and this new form of transport brought many problems to the riverside

PLATE 12 Life on a houseboat was one of the most delightful things imaginable (from a contemporary postcard)

PLATE 13 The Thames frozen at Cookham

PLATE 14 The fair sex punting at Bray during the summer flood of 1903

procession, carrying 'a capital string band', and the *Maidenhead Advertiser* reported that:

> ... the river was covered with hundreds of craft of all descriptions—boats, punts, canoes and steam launches, and these were decorated in most lavish style with lanterns, fairy lights or coloured fires, and as they moved down the course, the band meanwhile playing, the sight was one that must be seen to be realised.

Hundreds of pounds were spent on fireworks, Chinese lanterns, bucket lamps and fairy lights; lawns and eaves and flowerbeds were outlined, and lights were hung in trees or perhaps set to spell the names of riverside properties such as the bungalow Wigwam at Bourne End. Prizes offered for the best illuminated boats stimulated competition, and all sorts of ingenious ideas were put into practice. At Hampton Court and Ditton Venetian fête in 1890 an Eiffel Tower of massed lights floated down the stream. The winner at Bray the next year was a fully equipped schooner, with sails of tiny cardinal lamps and outlined with electric coloured lights. At Datchet in 1888 there was a Chinese pagoda with children in costume. At Marlow in various years were to be seen a dragon with fiery mouth emitting flames, at the head of a punt, a flaming cauldron, a sea serpent, an iceberg, a polar bear, and a man of war. At Bourne End a 'crocodile' opened and shut its ferocious mouth at intervals, the Earl of Yarmouth's canoe was decorated as a swan, and a launch represented the Man in the Moon. Bourne End's seventh regatta in 1903 was spoilt by poor weather, and the powerful organ of the steam circus, stationed too near the band of the East Surreys, failed to honour its promise not to play at the same time. But by the evening the weather cleared and the cares that infested the day were lost to memory as the military band, on two ballast punts roped together and illuminated by green lights, was taken in tow by the umpire's launch. Many small craft clustered around, attaching themselves to the band-boat.

Bourne End Venetian fête looked to the past in 1906, when the first prize was given to an electric launch representing a windmill and a water mill, the latter (outlined in red and white electric lamps) with a revolving wheel and ivy clinging to its walls. Two years later a punt designed as an airplane was vociferously applauded by the innocent inhabitants of that quiet little place who failed to recognise in it a symbol of the destruction of their world.

Cookham's Volunteer Fire Brigade, wearing their helmets and carrying blazing torches, mounted their manual fire engine, with life-sized wooden horses, on a huge ballast punt at the village's 1910 Venetian fête; the following year they put their fire escape against a canvas structure representing a house.

This was the age of tableaux vivants, often of a patriotic character, and they too were sometimes a feature of the scene. At Cookham in 1913 the prize for the launch class was given to a representation of St George and the Dragon. In 1900 an evening of songs and tableaux was arranged on the lawn opposite the church to raise money to pay a debt on the church heating apparatus. There were to be seen 'The Mistletoe Bough', 'Prince Charles' Farewell to Flora Macdonald', 'Tea and Scandal', 'How Happy Could I Be with Either' and, on a more serious note—to stir the imagination of those watching, to fill them with pride and bring to their minds a sense of achievement and high vocation—'The British Empire' and an illustration in three scenes of the well-loved song 'Comrades', including 'How He Won the VC'. A similar tableau under the title 'The Last Grip', in which a soldier defended his dying comrade against the enemy's attack, was shown after Maidenhead regatta in 1912; and the following year a true incident of the Matabele War, under the title 'The Last Stand', illustrated Major Wilson and a small party surrounded by the enemy, their last shot fired, dying singing the National Anthem. Most ironically, on the very brink of the precipice, a tableau of 'Peace' was shown that year, in which doves flew out behind uniformed men representing England, France, Russia and Germany.

Firework displays were complex and included all sorts of amazing spectacles, serious and comic. One year at Marlow, Port Arthur received a firework bombardment, and firework cocks fought. Another year there was a set-piece of Baden

Powell, and at Bourne End of Kitchener. Gymnastics and wrestling were seen at Bourne End; at Cookham a skeleton acrobat, fiery dragons, aerial jugglery, prismatic torrents, fiery cobras and a representation of Niagara Falls delighted spectators—thanks largely to the generosity of the proprietor of the Ferry Inn. War shells also were part of the display, watched with no premonitions of evil by parents whose baby sons sleeping safely at home—rounded cheeks against cot pillows in rush-lit nurseries, with comfortable nannies near to soothe the terrors of nightmare—were to be young men in 1914.

One of the grandest Venetian fêtes ever held on the river took place at Bray in 1891. Firework set-pieces eclipsing anything previously seen included a kicking donkey, men dancing a hornpipe, boxing, and a representation of the Battle of Trafalgar showing ships fighting and discharging cannon. The display came to an end as 11 o'clock chimed out from the grey church tower. Another grand occasion at Bray celebrated the return from New Zealand, where he had been aide-de-camp to Lord Onslow, of Mr James Guthrie, one of whose relations had taken the vicarage for the season. This was one of those occasions when dinner, served in a marquee to the guests, some of whom were drawn from the ranks of the aristocracy, was of a distinctly 'recherché' character. A firework Lottie Collins performing 'Ta-ra-ra-boom-de-ay' with particularly good leg action evoked roars of laughter; and it could be that some of the visitors, although breeding prohibited open guffaws, smiled under cover of darkness at the sight of a large sheep bearing emblazoned on its fore and hind quarters respectively portraits of Mr James Guthrie and Lord Onslow, and underneath the words 'New Zealand'.

River concerts originated at Cookham, apparently in 1887. As twilight thickened, the moon rose above the trees, and over the million twinkling lights on river and river bank the dome of night was jewelled with starshine, so a hush fell on the audience gathered on lawns and towpath or in boats slightly swaying to the motion of the current. A few tinkling notes, magnified by the water, sounded from the piano aboard the large ferry-punt moored in mid-stream which served as a concert platform, and then clear voices rang out into the darkness. Songs included Tosti's 'Beauty's Eyeṣ' and his 'Venetian Boat Song', 'Alice Where Art Thou?', 'The Lost Chord', 'I'll Sing Thee Songs of Araby', 'O Dry Those Tears', the 'Bedouin Love Song', 'Excelsior' and 'For Thee My Love', this last always sung by Colonel F. C. Ricardo, a well-known local figure. Sometimes tenor and baritone or tenor and soprano sang in duet, weaving patterns of harmony, as in 'O that We Two were Maying', or Benedict's 'The Moon Hath Raised her Lamp Above' from *The Lily of Killarney*. Gilbert and Sullivan was sung, and sometimes there were whistling solos. Patriotic songs were heard too— 'The Lads in Red' and 'Yes, Let Me like a Soldier Fall', the last accompanied by cornet obligato.

Comic songs were popular. The audience heard about the 'Three Little Niggers', the 'Putney 'Bus' and 'Muddled Maxims'; they were informed that by misfortune 'The Vlies be on the Turmeyuts', but were cheered to know that 'His 'art was true to 'is Poll'. The favourite was 'Razors', which was taken up by the audience. In 1891 river concerts were temporarily abandoned at Cookham because what had previously been a small local occasion had by then come to attract thousands of spectators from further away, and attempts of singers to make themselves heard were 'baulked and rendered nugatory by crackers, steam whistles, and the varied diversions of a tightly-packed crowd'. However, 'Razors' broke through, in response to insistent calls for melody, and the chorus was taken up by the various groups of spectators, each choosing its own key, words and style. These occasions were brought to an end by 'Auld Lang Syne' and the National Anthem, led from the ferry-punt which was brightly illuminated by electricity, taking its current from the electric launch *Loosestrife*.

Although river concerts flourished at Cookham and other places in the late 1800s, rather surprisingly Maidenhead did not follow suit until the beginning of the twentieth century. Could it have been because too insistent competition was feared from the iron monsters snorting and rattling through the night over Brunel's bridge? However this may be, once the custom was established there the gentle and tuneful songs of the age were heard, among them 'I Hear You Calling Me', 'Villia', 'Always', 'Two Eyes of Blue' and 'My Old Shako'. After the Engineers' and Fishermen's regatta in 1901, the launch the *Queen of the Thames* was moored almost in mid-stream for the concert, as an audience estimated at up to 4,000 listened from the banks and admired the illuminations brilliant against the night's blackness.

Professional artistes came down from London to perform at Maidenhead river concerts. Sometimes the programme was printed on fans, the sale of which in 1905 added about £10 to the regatta funds. The owner of West Court lent his riverside grounds, brilliantly illuminated by electricity from his newly installed plant, and there three years later a specially designed ship placed far up on the centre balcony of the house was outlined in Suterlite with the legend 'Good luck to the Regatta, 1908'. In 1911, hundreds stood on the lawn where in the cool, calm evening every word of the songs could be heard from the stage bordered with electric lights at the water's edge. A little girl danced 'The Tired Swan'. The following year it took a week to fit up the stage and illuminations at West Court, about 150 guests were present, and a sea of faces watched from the water where small craft were stationed at the front and launches behind so everyone had a clear view. The stage revolved to show the tableaux vivants to best advantage. When a tableau of Britannia was shown, all present sang 'Rule Britannia'. Just before the Great War a river concert was arranged at Marlow by Miss Eardley-Wilmot, who wrote 'My Little Grey Home in the West' and who lived with her father, Rear-Admiral Eardley-Wilmot, at the Old Malt House in St Peter's Street, Marlow.

But a new age was making its clamorous appearance. At the Maidenhead and Bray Watermen's regatta river concert in 1911 the songs included 'Susie and her Motor Bike'.

14

'MORE BARBAROUS THAN SCYTHED CHARIOTS'

The river cannot be considered in isolation. Just as much a part of the waterside scene as the visitors were the vehicles which took them to it, and the character of the riparian towns and villages was affected by the changing forms of transport to be seen there.

Earlier chapters showed how the railway opened up the reaches above lock. Some visitors arrived at the river on foot from the railway station, burdened with picnic hampers, while others arrived in smart private carriages driven by liveried coachmen. From time to time horses, those highly strung and sometimes unpredictable creatures, took fright at some sudden noise or unexpected sight, and bolted. On one occasion, for instance, a horse bolted after being alarmed by a launch's whistle, and the driver was thrown out and suffered a severe head wound.

Cabbies seem to have been a tough breed of men, not afflicted by humanitarian feelings when money was to be made. A letter in a *Lock to Lock Times* of 1888 pathetically describes cab horses as mere bags of bone, thrashed all the way to the station so that the driver might return for another fare, drawing a normal load of seven plus their driver, and working seven days a week. In 1905 a trough was erected near Maidenhead bridge where these unhappy creatures could pause a moment to cool their poor gasping muzzles. From time to time there were complaints about the squalor of the cabs, and 'Fleeced' complained to the *Maidenhead Advertiser* about exorbitant fares. These were half-a-crown from the station to Boulters (about 1½ miles) in 1904. Two people in the cab business wrote in reply defending these costs as necessary for them to make a living.

Cabs were a nuisance at Boulters, driving up and down

creating clouds of dust, and in 1894 arrangements were being made for a 'proper sanitary cab stand' to accommodate three of them there. There was fearful trouble between cabbies if fares were taken out of turn. On one occasion a cabbie who forced his way to the head of the queue offered to fight another who objected and, when the latter declared that 'he did not wish to disgrace himself with such a toe-rag', struck him twice in the face. Once there was a fight at Skindles— another place where competition was keen and a cab rank needed—and one driver forced the head of another through the hotel's window. Rival 'Jehus', as the *Maidenhead Advertiser* was wont to describe them, disagreed at the Boulters rank in 1909. One tried to push out of turn, whereupon the employer of another offered to fight the offender, calling him 'a —— scoundrel', 'making use of another offensive expression' and adding 'all your family are the same'. Sometimes cabbies used disgraceful language at Maidenhead station, and at the bridge in 1899 a Windsor cabbie not only failed to pay his toll but, putting his fingers to his nose, called the toll-house keeper 'a —— sod'.

When the bicycle craze swept England in later Victorian times, these vehicles were seen in their hundreds by the riverside. Henry Taunt, famous for his postcards of the Thames, had a two-seater tricycle on which his perspiring assistant sat in front busily pedalling while Taunt himself, very dignified, occupied the rear seat with his photographic equipment strapped between the axles.

At Maidenhead over the Easter holiday of 1882 'hundreds of alert travellers on spider-like wheels passed and re-passed daily through the principal thoroughfares', and on another occasion the 'furious' riding of bicycles and tricycles there was the theme of correspondence in the *Maidenhead Advertiser*.

'Lady cycling' was becoming very popular in the 1890s, and Mrs Grenfell was among those who took up this hobby. The *Maidenhead Advertiser* assured its readers that 'most of the fair sex pedal very gracefully, and there is nothing in the appearance of the ladies or the arrangement of their dress to offend the most fastidious'. But a few were to be seen passing through Maidenhead 'wearing knickers similar to those favoured by the sterner sex, except that they are of looser fit and hidden nearly to the knees by a coat, pinched in at the waist of like material'. A group of ladies in 'rational costume' excited the ridicule of spectators as they passed through Maidenhead on their way to Oxford in September 1897. Lady Jeune attacked this costume in outspoken terms, writing in *Badminton* magazine:

> No woman looks well in male attire . . . a woman is not made to wear tight-fitting apparel; when she puts it on she at once becomes ugly and mis-shapen. What can be more hideous than a collection of women of various sizes, shapes and weights, in the drab knickerbocker suit surmounted by the drab Tam o'Shanter hat? Women clothed like men, and 'unashamed', with their figures well bent over their machines, perspiring at every pore, their hair flying in the breeze (for your new woman-bicyclist does nothing by halves), present as ugly and as ridiculous a picture as one can imagine.

On Whit Monday evening 1897, 152 cycles crossed Maidenhead bridge in fifteen minutes. That year many people cycled to the Taplow Court fête where their machines were 'stabled' in a special marquee, and on Ascot Sunday 1905 hundreds were stacked by the riverside near Boulters. By the end of the nineteenth century Cookham bridge, where tolls were still payable, was reaping a handsome profit from cyclists, and the Thames Conservancy had to prohibit cycling on towpaths after 9am, special permission being necessary for those coaching boat crews. 'Scorchers' were the cause of this prohibition. Hundreds of cyclists had been going from Richmond bridge to Kingston bridge, then to the other bank from which they could reach Weybridge. Deaf old ladies and infirm old gentlemen with walking sticks trembled as bicycles rushed by with wildly ʌnkling bell or blowing bugle, and cab proprietors and people letting out boats grumbled because this new craze took away their business.

But then, above the bell and the bugle and the whirr of the wheel, above the jingle of harness, the clip-clop of hooves and the clatter of wheels, new sounds made themselves heard. 'Demoniac snorts, hooting and gurgling' caused horses to bolt, as, accompanied by 'squeaking, bellowing, tinkling, roaring or whistling with a piercing scream', clouds of dust appeared on the roads of riparian towns and villages. The noises ceased; the clouds of dust became stationary and slowly settled and in their settling revealed the symbols of another transport revolution, greater perhaps than any since the invention of the wheel. The age of the horseless carriage had arrived.

By the end of the century a nobleman who lived near Boulters was often to be seen 'on' his motor car by the river, and he was the single spy heralding the battalions which were to follow. The smart, moneyed people who took houses at Maidenhead for the season eagerly adopted this new method of transport, so that as early as 1902 there was quite a parade of motors by the river one spring Sunday, and on Ascot Sunday a great gathering of them. From then on things changed rapidly. The novelty ceased to be a novelty but increased, multiplied and predominated, had to be controlled and catered for, brought problems and regrets, danger and hatred in its wake. On Ascot Sunday 1904 there was a remarkable display of motors in the roads near Boulters, nearly a hundred being present at one time. The next year a party of actors and actresses, having supped in the West End after the theatres closed one Saturday night, travelled down to Maidenhead in a cavalcade of eight cars to spend the rest of the weekend at the Riviera Hotel. The Honourable C. S. Rolls in a Rolls-Royce led the way from Piccadilly—deserted then but for 'a convocation of tired policemen'—along country lanes and past villages, through the sweet-scented night, to where a small crowd waited to greet and cheer them as they crossed the bridge.

The King arrived to visit Taplow Court wearing goggles, although the motor car he travelled in was 'glass-protected'. But Lord Desborough was slow to take up the new craze, perhaps because of his love of horses and great skill in driving them. On Ascot Sunday 1906 there were sixty-two motors in Skindles garage and an adjoining meadow, many on the Riviera lawn, and twelve lined up under a wall in a road near Boulters. As the years went on, miles of parked cars filled roads adjacent to the river on Ascot Sundays. The term 'parked' came to be accepted in common parlance, and ceased to appear in inverted commas in the *Maidenhead Advertiser*. The huge influx of traffic presented a major problem to the police, short delays caused long queues, and several times a sergeant or constable shouted to his superior, 'Look out, sir! You'll be knocked down!' Mounted police controlled motor traffic near the bridge. Skindles garage was advertised as letting taxi-cabs—'magnificent new cars, smart drivers in uniform'—at 1s per mile and 3s per hour for waiting. Huge numbers of motors passed through Maidenhead at Henley regatta time, and increasing numbers of guests travelled by car to the annual banquet at Taplow Court. One Ascot Sunday there was a great deal of dust as watering carts were unable to get through the heavy traffic, 'and policemen and others were transformed for the nonce into millers'. By 1913 it was decided not to allow motors to wait for any length of time on the riverside promenade, and the problem of congestion was further eased as a meadow near the Thames Hotel was offered for Sunday parking. Blackbirds and thrushes sang in ivy-covered willows nearby and the small parking charges collected to the sound of their sweet notes were to be given to good causes. By 1914 twenty extra police from other parts of the country were required to regulate the Ascot Sunday traffic.

Motor cars, like bicycles, affected the amount of business done by cabbies. They affected Henley's trade at regatta time, for people who used to stay a week now came down daily bringing luncheon baskets. Elsewhere, the demand for furnished apartments fell off. Thousands of stablemen, coachmen and grooms saw their jobs disappear. There was an important sale at Skindles of carriages and driving equipment, the owner of which was giving up the livery and bait business to make room for an extra motor garage. Motor cars were becoming a great industry. The *Morning Post* reported that many launch owners had given up their boats for cars, for 'having tasted the joys of speed' they found river travel too slow. An American observer was of the opinion that they were destroying English home life; and the daughter of a

Mr Farrar of Cookham Dean eloped with her father's chauffeur.

This new form of transport created widespread bitterness. For the first time in history machines brought danger to the highways and byways of England—to men and women and children, to dogs and birds and hedgehogs, and to a myriad of small furred creatures. Properties on main roads depreciated in value, their windows permanently closed against clouds of dust, and formerly green hedgerows were coated with it. The vicar of Bisham complained of the noise made in his village by the hooting of a motor car known locally as 'the Sick Giant'— a 'peculiarly disgusting' sound which disturbed invalids whose bedrooms abutted onto the road. A Twyford doctor wrote to the *Daily Telegraph* of 'moneyed oafs and titled cads' in cars, of the dust and smell which made health impossible and beautiful gardens a thing of the past. He suggested that it would be better to have trains on roads, for then one would know at what time to get out of the way. Two wheels went over the little daughter of a waterman when she ran in front of a car in Eton High Street, and a child died on the main road at Hurley. A letter to the *Maidenhead Advertiser* suggested that drivers should be hanged for causing death. A well-known Maidenhead resident involved in a motor accident at Boulters only escaped with his life by a miracle, and a road junction near the lock was described as a veritable death-trap. In 1910 the cottage women of Great Britain prepared a pathetic appeal to be sent to the Queen. They wrote:

May it please Your Majesty: the village women of the United Kingdom humbly beseech Your Majesty to help us get some relief from the motor-cars. We are sure Your Majesty cannot know how much we suffer from them. They have made our lives a misery. Our children are always in danger, our things are ruined by the dust, we cannot open our windows, and our rest is spoiled by the noise at night . . .

Riverside towns and villages making fat profits from the wealthy classes now in the grip of the motor-car craze were in danger of losing their custom if they made strenuous efforts to curb speeding. In 1907, for instance, when Cookham Rural

District Council were trying to bring in a 10mph speed limit in certain places, a motorist suggested as retaliation a boycott of local tradesmen, a move which had already proved successful in Andover. A letter to the *Maidenhead Advertiser* pointed out that fining motorists for speeding was not the way to attract residents, and 'the class of people we wish to attract are buying motors as fast as the works can turn them out'. Another correspondent saw hotels suffering if harsh fines frightened away motorists. By 1911 Maidenhead's main roads were being tar-macadamed because of the greatly increased traffic.

For a decade after the first appearance of the motor car at Boulters lock, the *Maidenhead Advertiser* continued to ring with denunciations of 'the hideous figures enveloped in hearth-rugs and burglar-masks' and the machines they drove, variously described as 'engines of iniquity', 'perfect Juggernauts, spreading death and destruction in their wake', 'racing chaff-cutting machines', 'engines of Hades', and 'tearing, screeching, dust-raising, stinking motors'. Mr F. T. Wethered, the vicar of Hurley, with a vision always before his eyes of a little boy's body broken beyond repair on the main road there, resolved to vote only for anti-motor MPs who would pledge themselves to abolish 'these damnable engines of Satan, more barbarous than scythed chariots'.

15

HOUSEBOATS

Life on a luxurious houseboat—with the galley and servants' quarters perhaps on a lesser boat adjacent—was the pleasantest thing imaginable. From the moment the occupants opened their eyes in the morning to the sight of sunlight glinting through willow leaves on to the river's placid waters, to the moment they closed them at night to the sight of those same trees with star-gems entangled in their branches, they experienced all the comfort of fashionable life without its irksome restraints. They exchanged grey London streets for the yielding Thames; hard-faced London houses for meadow, hill, woodland and stands of rustling trees, and pavements for towpaths where the dog-rose grew. They heard birdsong from leafy pastures, the plashing of oars, and, mingling perhaps with their dreams, the strange faint gobbling sound made by feeding swans.

Fred. S. Thacker, a great authority on the river Thames, wrote in his *General History of the River*, published in 1914, that the earliest mention he had found of the ancestor of the houseboat, a barge equipped as a country house, was of one at Richmond in 1780. By the time these floating homes reached their heyday in later Victorian times, they had achieved standards of luxury which the most exacting hedonist could not fault, and one at least of them displayed a sophistication, a garishly ostentatious announcement of its owner's wealth, not quite of a piece with the simplicity of its rustic surroundings. This was the *Satsuma*, described by the *Lock to Lock Times* as a monster houseboat, which was built at Hampton in 1888. The main saloon was 750sq ft, with six bedrooms opening out of it, two of them 10ft by 12ft. The windows were filled with bevelled plate glass containing stained glass squares with flower, bird and fruit patterns. The top deck was 20ft above river level. The whole thing could be taken to pieces, and indeed this was necessary if it was to pass through locks. There were two pianos on board; the dining saloon was illuminated by lamps with elaborate shades, the table covered with a deep-fringed cloth, chairs with studded backs placed in position round it, and valuable Satsuma vases displayed on the sideboard (and more in the bedrooms). The original owner forbade smoking on board, but under a new owner, as if to bear out the preacher of Ecclesiastes, this remarkable vessel was consumed by flames.

Houseboat advertisements appeared in the *Lock to Lock Times*. One to let had seven beds, plate, linen, a piano, awning from end to end, and a dinghy; another had cellars (sic) and a full-sized bath; a third, 'pretty and well furnished', was offered complete with the services of its owner, a naval pensioner, who would act as steward. The *Water Lily* was equipped with two saloons with fireplaces and parquet floors, electric bells, hot and cold water, and a good servant's bedroom. *Little Billee*, sleeping eight, could be hired for 80 guineas for Henley week. No less than 200 guineas was asked for the regatta period for a houseboat described as large, palatial and beautifully furnished throughout, with a tender containing a large kitchen and three servants' bedrooms, two of them ready equipped with a cook and housemaid respectively. The Prowse Launch and Boat Agency undertook not only to hire houseboats for Henley but also to provision them, and could generally provide servants used to river life. Mr and Mrs Pennell, an American couple who described their journey down the Thames in *The Stream of Pleasure* which appeared in 1891, noted 'white-capped maids . . . busy with brooms and buckets'.

At Shiplake, lock vendors of fruit and vegetables did a good trade, houseboats taking the opportunity to supplement their stocks. The *Lock to Lock Times* calculated the aggregate domestic expenditure of all these vessels in 1891 as close on £1,000 per week, and was of the opinion that they should patronise not London stores but local tradesmen.

The feminine influence was apparent in the adornment of houseboats, for each had its colour scheme, with flowers carefully chosen to match or blend. Mrs Annie Smith, who was at Marlow regatta in the *Bohemia* in 1890, stole a march on other owners, for her boat's scarlet curtains were shown off not only by its snow-white awnings, but also by her white poodle, 'said to be the finest specimen extant'. The colour scheme of the *Rouge et Noir* is explained by its name. The *Dolce Far Niente* had peacock-blue flower-boxes and vases, and cathedral-glass windows. In the late 1880s it was fashionable to decorate houseboat walls with Japanese and other fans and handscreens, but by Edwardian days furnishings and ornaments were less flamboyant afloat, as on land.

An illustration called 'A Houseboat Reception' appeared in the *Lock to Lock Times* in 1891. It showed a lady wearing a fur wrap being handed from a canoe and received by her host who was in the act of raising his hat in greeting. Although this particular guest was clearly the essence of gentility, it was not unknown for owners to get 'fast ladies' on board and make so much noise that they disturbed the slumbers of the long-suffering riparian householder. A houseboat featured in a divorce case in 1889. Its owner (the co-respondent, a theatrical costumier) was overheard talking in suspicious circumstances to the wife of one of his guests, after which the deceived husband chanced to notice his host beating an undignified retreat out of the window. This took place at Maidenhead, a town often featured in fashionable divorce cases. Sundry well known people were to be seen going through Boulters with partners to whom their vows of fidelity, if any, had been of a purely unofficial character; but Turner in his wisdom found his memory of their names curiously elusive when detectives later arrived to question him. His memory was never at fault, though, if he recognised a burglar.

Houseboats were by no means exclusively the province of the wealthy and the grand. In 1883 the *Daily Telegraph* pointed out the pleasures of bachelor life aboard one of these floating homes. Three or four young men would pool their resources to hire one for the summer, travelling daily to their City offices from some convenient station such as Reading or Staines and returning, hot and exhausted, to the cool evening river. Then, having abandoned the responsibility of being looked after by servants, they would prepare their meal, and sit on deck as the stars came out, chatting in a desultory way as the slow smoke curled from their pipes into the darkening air.

In earlier years small colonies of artists led this idyllic life, their subjects ready-made in the beautiful scenes surrounding them. In 1891, after the death of Keeley Halswelle, owner of the houseboat the *Kelpie* moored by Cleeve lock, a tribute in *The Hawk* recalled: 'Those were golden summers, in the years before the Thames became a Cockney's Paradise, when, under the elm trees in Pangbourne Reach, used to be moored the little fleet of houseboats, whose owners formed such a festive little coterie.' Vicat Cole was among their number. G. D. Leslie recalled Alma-Tadema coming down to see Sir Henry Thompson whose vessel was anchored off Bisham (another favourite place for artists) and how they sat on the deck sketching away together. Hurley too was a popular mooring place for brethren of the brush.

The *Lock to Lock Times* of 1891 informed readers:

> The number of journalists, novelists, and dramatists, who seek inspiration and an undisturbed working place in Lockland is large; and it is safe to say that some of the best reading which will be served up in the Christmas numbers at the end of the year, will be written in house-boats moored in shady places, or in retreats whose windows overlook the river, during the coming summer.

George Edwardes the theatrical impresario had a houseboat, the *Periwinkle*, on which he had 'accorded full liberty and licence to the profession' the previous year—a curiously ambiguous statement, but presumably to be taken in its innocuous sense as the *Lock to Lock Times* expressed a hope that his hospitality would be repeated in 1891.

Although the *Daily Telegraph* assured its bachelor readers in 1883 that riparian owners 'if courteously solicited' would generally let houseboats moor by their property, the following year one such owner was complaining to the Select Committee on Thames River Preservation about the length of time they stayed in position, which was quite a new thing. Houseboats paid no rents or taxes but destroyed the privacy of those who did, whose gardens chanced to border the river.

PLATE 15 A crowded scene in Cookham lock, showing steamers in the background, *c*1895

PLATE 16 The gondola belonging to Abney House, Bourne End, the home of Mr C. Hammersley. The gondolier was Giulio

PLATE 17 The Oxford boat race crew at Abney House, Bourne End

PLATE 18 The Abney House ladies' eight, with their cox

In 1885 the Thames Preservation Act already referred to limited mooring.

The Thames. Putney to Cricklade explains the decline of the houseboat. This decline was partly caused by restrictions at Henley regatta. Watching the races from club lawns became increasingly popular, while the growing use of the motor car by society people in the new century made them not only more mobile but more restless. Renting bungalows was cheaper and gave the pleasure of riverside life combined with the convenience of being on land. But a houseboat was a world of its own, and life on board offered a unique charm which retained the loyalty of a staunch body of afficionados.

A rather surprising outburst was printed in the *St James's Gazette* in 1891, in which the houseboat was styled 'that most hideous invention of this latter age—that polluter of the waters—that blot on the landscape'. And indeed, in 1886 a *Lancet* commissioner found in the refuse from one houseboat at Henley:

> ... a great number of decomposing salad leaves, some rotten fruit, innumerable egg shells, with part of the yellow of the eggs still adhering, several large pieces of bread, the skin of a salmon, a skirt of lamb, stale pieces of fat and meat, some spring onions, innumerable crushed lemons, faded flowers, lobster shells, bruised tomatoes, and a dead roach.

A bucketful of water taken from the midst smelt, he declared (being, it is evident, a gentleman not given to hyperbole), very unpleasant.

'The loveliest thing that is a shadow hath.'

16

POLLUTION

In 1794 a freeholder of the Thames had objected to the making of locks and weirs as obstructions to the river's function as a natural sewer. Luckily this somewhat idiosyncratic view did not prevail during the Golden Age of the Thames.

Impurities fell into two categories: sewage; and other matter either thrown in or permitted to reach the Thames from tributaries. Cut river weeds, if allowed to remain in the water, could become obstructions and cause pollution, and in 1891, under the Thames Conservancy Act, some men were prosecuted who had allowed weeds to flow down from the river Lambourn. Empty bottles bobbed about in the current. G. D. Leslie saw them floating on Henley waters, emptied of their champagne and flung in at regatta time, and with them straw bottle-cases and paper, while corks by the bushel were to be found in eddies below any large town. Lord Desborough complained at a Thames Conservancy meeting in 1912 of rubbish thrown into the river, where strawberries and lettuce formed a 'messy mass' in some places. Conservancy officials were empowered to inspect launches and from time to time prosecuted when rubbish and ashes from houseboats caused pollution; and when filter beds intended to prevent soapsuds entering the river at Bray proved unsatisfactory, the Conservancy asked for them to be cleaned and replaced. In 1887 a river keeper was 'actively engaged in removing dead animals' which had met a watery death.

Fish were endangered or killed by various substances, sickened by sheep washing done in tributaries, and killed en masse from the Buckinghamshire Wye to the Thames in 1897, when poisonous liquid pumped from the High Wycombe gas works into the town's sewers seeped through the waterlogged sewage farm. Even earthworms died then, as the vicious poison entered their dark and loamy beds. Although the Thames Conservancy had powers over tributaries for a certain distance from where they joined the river, it was possible for waste matter to reach it from higher up, and uncomfortable sidelong glances were cast at china clay used in paper manufacture on the Wye. The motor car too caused pollution of the Thames, for increasingly roads were tarred to strengthen them against wear such as they had never before suffered and to banish the clouds of dust tormenting other road users and nearby residents. As a consequence objectionable matter, consisting of tarry substances and oil, was brought into the river by surface drains, while lubricating oil from steamers and motor boats also floated on the waters.

From 1866 the duty of controlling pollution of the river was imposed by government on the Thames Conservancy, and their authority in this respect was later extended to the catchment area. The hygienic disposal of sewage imposed great financial burdens on riparian towns but action was essential, for by the mid 1860s, Thacker wrote, sewage was accumulating in locks, sometimes in such quantities that it had to be removed at considerable expense before the gates could be opened. Above Teddington lock at this time it was reported to be 'six inches thick, and as black as ink'. Maidenhead in early days, as stated by its own newspaper, used to advertise its presence by its smell; and as late as 1888 cottagers were still wont to empty 'utensils' into a stream running to the river there, a practice which was to be forbidden forthwith. Taunt, in *A New Map of the River Thames from Oxford to London*, based on surveys taken in 1871 and including a guide, complained of the influx of a disgraceful open sewer below Wallingford bridge, and Leslie reported some years later the presence of a 'small ugly black archway' by the Royal Park at Windsor, through which 'the sewage from the town or Castle found its way, in an entirely unsophisticated condition, right into the river . . . Yet here were quite a number of men in punts fishing for roach, which low-minded fish is taken in great quantities at this spot.'

Sewage works were built up and down the river in the last

quarter of the nineteenth century. Wallingford in 1890 was 'at last bestirring itself to remedy its drainage system, and none too soon', and similar plans were in train at Newbury from whence sewage travelled down the Kennet to the Thames. Henley's new sewage works attracted a visit from the Inventors' Institute in 1888, and Abingdon, Oxford, Reading, Maidenhead, Windsor and Faringdon (the last on account of its position on a tributary) sooner or later dipped deep into their municipal purses to sweeten air and water. Even at Hampton Court, where for three and a half centuries Wolsey's drainage channels had functioned with an efficiency which made it a model for all lesser places, alterations were made in 1871 to withdraw the outfall from the river.

Windsor's new works cost well over £40,000; Oxford and Reading were thought to have spent over £2,000,000; Maidenhead's outlay on alterations and additions was £40,000. Despite the large sums paid, these systems were not always efficient in their early days, and towns received warnings from the Thames Conservancy, or had to pay nominal fines. The Conservancy learnt to act with patience and diplomacy, as indeed it had to, for the new legislation created resentment—not in the towns, where the benefits of pure water were immediately apparent and brought profit to those inhabitants who made or supplemented their incomes from the summer visitors, but in small places high up the Thames or its tributaries, where villagers resented being put to trouble and expense for the sake of Thames-side hoteliers, or to enable the Conservancy to make a healthy income from the London water companies. Sturdy peasants ensconced in remote settlements, and accustomed all their lives, as their fathers before them, to fling noxious matter into the streams which chattered so gaily past their doors and swept impurities away to the great river, did not welcome the appearance of perspiring and complaining officials on bicycles.

But by determination, perseverance, tact, and as much leniency as was consistent with duty, the Conservancy turned the Thames into a pure river. It did not exercise its power over tributaries where it felt there was an intention to comply with legislation, and in the first four years of its extended

authority obtained only eighteen convictions. By the end of
that time pollution had been diverted in forty-four cases
where property owners had been contacted, and from
seventy-eight towns and villages on tributaries, besides
which the Conservancy was in touch with further district
councils and property owners. In 1887 water supplied to the
water companies was pronounced clear and bright, containing exceptionally little organic matter. Mr Grenfell described
the Thames in 1898 as the purest river in Europe, and by 1913
the *Maidenhead Advertiser* pronounced that the new
processes which had come into use had increased the purity of
its water a thousand times. All this was fortunate for those
who not only washed in the Thames but drank it. A *Punch*
cartoon showed a boating man patiently waiting at the front
door of a lock-keeper's cottage for the return of the water
bottle which he had handed in. Meanwhile it was being filled
from the river at the back.

17

HOTELS

The following appeared in *Truth* in 1894:

I was much struck the other day by the following announcement among the bankruptcy adjudications in *The Times*—'Bruce, George William Thomas Brudenell, Marquis of Ailesbury (deceased), who is domiciled in England, and resides at Skindles Hotel, Taplow'. Many are the privileges of peers. Can it be one of them is that when an eminent nobleman dies he goes to Skindles?

Skindles, by Maidenhead bridge, was the most famous hotel of the Golden Age of the Thames and, like Maidenhead itself, was made by the railway. In earlier days it was known as the Orkney Arms, taking its name from the then owner of Taplow Court, and was distinguished by nothing in particular from any other riverside inn well positioned by a coaching road. The original Skindle began life as a boy in a posting-yard and progressed to become postillion, and later under-butler, to Lord Carlisle. Then he became head waiter at the Sun Inn, Maidenhead, married the landlord's niece, took another inn in the town and also became a coach proprietor. When the Great Western Railway reached Slough, by which time he was proprietor of the Orkney Arms, 'the business turned topsy-turvy'. He and his son approached Sir Robert Harvey, the owner of some riverside coal wharves then lying idle, who agreed to lay out money on the hotel. New premises were erected. Skindle had given no thought to the question of what sign he would adopt, and when approached on the subject replied, 'Call it Skindles'. His son, a noted river man in his day and skilled with the punt-pole, succeeded to the business, and finally retired from the town in 1873.

Skindles, a great haunt of the Brigade of Guards in its early years, was also patronised by Prince Tum-tum, whose

favourite lunch was a mutton chop and a little brandy and
soda—probably multiplied. By 1875 the new proprietor, a Mr
Lewis, a 'thorough piscator' and honorary secretary of the
local Thames Angling Preservation Society, was running a 6d
omnibus in summer from Taplow station. An article in *The
World* about Sunday at Maidenhead in 1877 described dinner
at Skindles as consisting of 'clear asparagus soup, whitebait
crisp as at Greenwich, and the famous ducklings of Ayles-
bury' with dry champagne. On at least one Sunday in 1880
the hotel was crowded from basement to attic, and by 1885
the frontage had been altered, the white facing removed to
reveal red brickwork. Maidenhead, as already mentioned,
had a lively reputation in the divorce courts, and scandal
touched Skindles about this time when the manager of a
detective agency was charged with having solicited a Post
Office clerk to disclose the contents of a telegram addressed to
a lady staying there.

The upper classes flocked to Skindles, but it was not
unknown for lesser mortals to experience its recherché
qualities, for in 1894 the Maidenhead and Bray Watermen
held their annual dinner there, after which the piccolo, that
Jenny Wren among instruments, sounded a piping solo, and
from the watermen's weatherbeaten faces came songs brimful
of the sentiment never far under the Victorian surface,
gentling the condition of the roughest: 'I'll Stand by my
Friend', 'The Patriotic Tramp', 'The Midshipmite', and 'My
Pretty Jane'.

The Thames Valley was often afflicted by winter floods, and
in 1903 all who lived by the river trade suffered an unpre-
cedented blow in the form of a summer flood. This affected
Skindles less than other hotels for motorists came there to see
that remarkable spectacle; so at luncheon time 'there was not
that huge waste of chicken and ducks which had pretty well
ruined some riverside larders for the season'. A couple of
summers afterwards the proprietor, alert to business, invited
representatives of the press to the hotel to display the beauty
of the district to them and to 'demonstrate that the reports of
the recent floods were very much exaggerated'. About thirty
reporters from most of the leading London journals travelled

down in a special railway carriage, were driven to visit local beauty spots, and at Skindles met the mayor of Maidenhead, as well as Mr Grenfell—who replied to the toast 'The River Thames' by talking about the work of the Thames Conservancy—and a regular visitor from Manchester who enthused about the locality. They noted the new 'gorgeously-appointed dining-saloon':

> Spacious, well-lighted, elaborately decorated, comfortably furnished, looking out on to the rippling water . . . an ideal luncheon or banqueting-room, and as one sits therein discussing the products of Skindles' kitchen and cellar, the charming parterres of Bridge House on the Berkshire shore, the moving craft on the broad river, the weeping willows in the foreground, and the fine stone-bridge, can all be taken in at a glance.

In the afternoon they went on the river in one of Skindles' electric launches, after which they returned to urban things, bearing to thronging London pavements thronging visions of the Thames' placid beauty.

Riverside hotels were built or rebuilt, extended and modernised during late Victorian days to cater for the vastly increased traffic, and others besides G. D. Leslie sighed for the quaint hostelries of earlier times. Arthur T. Pask, whose facetious book *A Playful Guide to the Thames from Teddington to Oxford* pre-dated *Three Men in a Boat* by some few years, praised the parlour in the Barley Mow at Clifton Hampden as likely to appeal to those who admired old-fashioned places and enjoyed bumping their heads against ceilings, and he deplored the new fashion of spoiling old Thames inns by covering them with stucco. The Thames innkeeper, he complained, wanted:

> . . . to keep pace with the times and have his place chock-full of cads and rowdies. They are sticking up brand-new beer-engines, and gas-fittings and suchlike all along the river now, and seem to forget that half the charm of doing the river is resting in the queer old shanties that have held their own for three or four centuries.

But at this early date a number of hotels survived in their ancient picturesqueness. At the Lamb at Wallingford an old-fashioned bar stood to one side of the large coach entrance, and a parlour to the other, while joints hung overhead 'as gracefully as the grape festoons in the chromos of Italy'. At the Swan at Streatley, 'the prettiest and quaintest of little hostelries, there is a brand-new piano, and the passages are so dark and narrow and wooden that you fancy yourself inside a prison hulk . . .'; while spittoons still stood on the sanded floor of the White Hart at Sonning.

The Royal River, which appeared shortly after Pask's book, gives glimpses of other tempting riverside inns. The Trout at Godstow with its rose-scented garden retained 'all its characteristics of creepers, flowers, tiled roof, and pleasant water-side seats'. The Beetle and Wedge above Streatley was:

> . . . a quaint, three-gabled old place, overgrown with ivy and shaded by clumps of luxuriant elms . . . its brick-floored parlour a cool retreat from the glare of the outer world. There is usually a garrulous villager or two, in the long-descended smock-frock beloved of the older generation of peasants even in these changeful days.

The Bells of Ouseley was described as 'perfectly free, at present, from modern revivalism, and from all manner of conscious style . . . Its quaint bow-windows, one on either side of a porch entered by way of a steep flight of steps—the wholesome dread of unsteady topers'; the only reminder of a later age being the bicycles often to be found resting against the walls of the old stone stable previously occupied only by stamping and snorting horses rolling the whites of their eyes at intruders into its dusky dim interior.

G. D. Leslie thought the Ferry Inn at Cookham first-rate. He stayed in a little front bedroom there one October night, and in the morning his poetic spirit responded to the scene beyond his window: 'the mist curling up from the water, and the autumnal sun lighting up the Cliveden beeches radiant in golden glory'. Krausse, whose *A Pictorial History of the River Thames* came out in 1889, shared Leslie's nostalgia for the Compleat Angler's earlier days when during the reign of Mrs Parslow it was 'the most delightful riverside resort on the Thames, being an old-fashioned, rambling, one-storied building, with a gabled roof and quaint chimney stacks', now 'metamorphosed into a modern hotel, the buxom waitress abolished in favour of the swallow-tailed waiter, and the bread-and-cheese fare exchanged for the modern *entrée*'.

Mr Wellington Wack, whom we last saw opening his eyes wide at the sights to be seen in a Teddington backwater, brought a brisk transatlantic viewpoint to English inns in the early twentieth century:

> . . . somehow they remain the same from one decade to another— rusty, inefficient, comfortless, and proud, disdaining modern hygienic apparatus, the art of cooking, the wisdom of conforming to modern taste. There are rare exceptions . . . There are a few— only a few—inns in the Thames valley where hospitality is still genuine, where a welcome is graciously warmed with good port from the wood, where the hostess has the genius of home in what she does, and where the host has the courage to look over and beyond the wall which surrounds his nation's snug little island.

The Compleat Angler met with the approval of this very demanding critic:

> The centre entrance hall contains many rare specimens of large trout caught near the inn during the last forty years. An old hat tree of stags' hoofs and horns and many other trophies adorn the niches. The bar is a tiny tap room, quite in its original form and inconvenience, and the dining room beyond is unlike anything on the river, its glass sides and front affording a view, through willows, of the weir, pool, lock, and river channel. This is a spacious room with a low ceiling, and practically overhangs the whirlpool and cascade whose liquid cadence is never stilled . . . The menu is intelligently chosen, the cuisine excellent and the service courteous and precise.

The beds, too, he praised, pronouncing them 'unlike English beds, for they were fat and crisp and without the varicose lumps and flabby linen so common in all bedchambers from Bow to Belgravia'.

Mr Wellington Wack must surely have approved of at least one aspect of the Caversham Bridge Hotel—a reproduction half timbered building recently enlarged and possessing two tennis courts—for there the public were assured 'the sanitary arrangements' were 'under the newest improved system'. Other hotels boasted other innovations. By 1890 both the Ray Mead at Maidenhead and the White Hart at Windsor proudly advertised themselves as lighted by electricity throughout; and the latter, all unwitting that the age of the horse was dying, demolished its old stables and erected new ones to hold 75 horses, with a carriage floor for 60 carriages, and 16 bedrooms for servants and grooms. Temperance hotels at Abingdon and Reading about this time compensated for their inability to warm the inner man by their ability to cleanse the outer man, for both were advertised as having bathrooms. Cliveden Temperance Hotel had a photographic chamber. By 1891 the French Horn at Sonning and the Bells of Ouseley had been re-decorated and 'improved', and, under the reign of Mr Foottit at the Compleat Angler, various extensions had been made including the addition of ten extra bedrooms and a billiard room. The Ray Mead had also expanded.

Within sight of Tilehurst's small station two buildings stood side by side, witness in bricks and mortar to changing times, changing tastes and changing patronage. They were the old and the new Roebuck inns, and A. J. Church was familiar with both of them. The new one he described as: 'now a handsome hostelry, with spacious dining-saloons, a printed *menu*, a wine *carte* with some thirty vintages upon it at fashionable prices'. But thirty or so years before, the Roebuck had been just a roadside public house, where he had stayed in a quaint bedroom with yellow-washed walls and low ceiling, and primitive lattices not too used to opening. 'The old building still stands unchanged by the side of its fashionable successor; and dusty drovers on their way to Reading market rest, as of old, under the elms before the door; but the river-side inn as I knew it in my youth is no more.'

At Aston, near Rememham, downstream from Henley, a new bright red inn was erected. This was the Flower Pot, much frequented by fishermen. The Pennells put up there, and, from beneath the large terracotta flower pot which was the inn's sign, looked on 'elms, the loveliest in the whole length and breadth of England', which met over the narrow lanes bordered with fields of fiery poppies, while nearby there were to be seen old-fashioned gardens 'full of weary sunflowers waiting to count the steps of the sun that would not shine'.

The Quarry Hotel on Cockmarsh at Bourne End was built in the late 1880s and got its licence in 1888 despite local objections, including those of the Ferry Hotel and the churchwardens of Cookham church. In 1901 the Crown, overlooking Cookham Moor, was rebuilt as 'one of the most commodious and convenient and luxuriously furnished hotels in the district'—gabled, balconied, and complete with mahogany bar fittings and Maples furnishings.

Two new large hotels were erected at Maidenhead during this period. Mr H. Woodhouse, whose ancestors slept in Bray churchyard under lichened tombstones, the oldest dating back to the sixteenth century, was a prosperous boat-builder who expanded into the hotel business. His Thames Hotel was erected in the late 1880s and considered gigantic with twenty-five bedrooms. In 1896 it was advertised as having an electric fire escape. By 1898 the building was mature, its outline softened by creepers on balcony and window, and had achieved even more mammoth proportions, with 'thirty lofty and convenient bedrooms, suites of private apartments' and a photographic dark room. It had a telegraph office and multitudes of distinguished visitors including Princess Fredericka of Hanover and 'peers galore'. The Riviera by Maidenhead bridge was for some time a huge white elephant. It was originally built as a mansion which the owner intended to let, but having failed to do so, in 1889 he sought a licence, wishing to turn it into a first-class hotel with no less than thirty-six bedrooms. The clergy of Maidenhead petitioned against his application, as did Mr Woodhouse, who said that despite the fact that the season had been a good one, he had only had to turn people away three times. He could hardly live, his prices were not too high, but on the contrary low, and he could not tell if another bad season would 'knock him out of time'. Cynical laughter greeted these remarks, but the Riviera did not get its licence. By 1891, it appears, all was well, for the Riviera was by then open, having been elaborately furnished at a cost of well over £2,000.

The Packhorse at Staines was rebuilt during this period, D'Oyley Carte built a fine new hotel at Shepperton, the inn at Thames Ditton was considerably 'brushed up', and at Richmond the old Star and Garter, a dignified Georgian building, was replaced by a Victorian palace, attached to which was the Pavilion containing a ballroom. This hotel could feed a thousand at a time, and had of course the advantage of Richmond's famous view.

Despite the large profits which good seasons brought, the lives of hoteliers were fraught with worries and difficulties, and sometimes circumstances got the better of them. In 1904 the proprietor of the Quarry Hotel at Bourne End, who had already suffered from two floods during his two years there, had a disastrous season and was unable to pay his debts. In 1910 even the prosperous Woodhouse was insolvent, blaming his failure on 'bad debts and bad seasons' and the motor car which had caused his trade to fall off as people tended to go farther afield. The Ray Mead Hotel also became bankrupt about this time, as did the Manor Hotel at Datchet. The latter's trade had been adversely affected not only by the 222 wet days of the previous season, but by the departure of houseboats from Datchet Reach after residents had complained of the noise made by some occupants.

We now come to the vexed question of overcharging. The hotelier had only a short season in which to make his profit, and, as an editorial in the *Lock to Lock Times* pointed out with humour typical of the period: 'The majority of up-river houses, we believe, have long since found it to their best interests to welcome the coming, but not *bleed* the parting guest.' Complaints reached the magazine. One correspondent wrote of being charged 8s with 3s attendance for a double-bedded room with coffee and bread and butter in the morning. ('Stiff, very!') At the Compleat Angler, which was described in 1888 as 'rather a warm place to stay at', 3s was charged for tea with bread, butter and jam, and both the waiter and the customer were said to have blushed at the sight of the bill. A *Punch* cartoon showed a waiter in pirate's costume holding a flint-lock pistol at a customer's head. In

1905 the Ray Mead Hotel was successfully sued for overcharging.

But hoteliers suffered too. It was not unknown for people taking their own food to expect to borrow cutlery free of charge. At Abingdon about 1891, four rowing men with gargantuan appetites sat down to a 14½lb joint of beef, leaving not enough for a meal for one. The charge was 5s a head, and 'the waitress gave one astonished glance at the table and fled to her mistress'. The invention of the telephone eased hoteliers' problems, for it enabled them to ring up for supplies at the last minute, instead of having to order in advance not knowing if a weekend would be fine or wet. Hotels were among the earliest buildings to install telephones, and the number of Skindles, for instance was '4, Maidenhead'.

But those days lay in the future when Mr Foottit of the Compleat Angler expressed himself on the class of people frequenting the river. They were not great, he said, nor were they likely to improve, adding that most hotel visitors grumbled on principle, and 'if you gave them ambrosia they would say it was the other article'.

18

RIVER TRIPS

The advertisement for the Abbey Hotel, Medmenham, concluded with the following unequivocal statement: 'Bean-feasts NOT catered for'.

The *Maidenhead Advertiser* too regarded such excursions with a severe eye, reserving its most solemn strictures for the Grand Order of Water Rats—music hall artistes whose conduct on a steamer trip in 1904 was, readers were informed, no credit to their profession. 'River habitués', we are given to understand, did 'not always appreciate the visits of these Londoners'. But for all such indignation, real or feigned, what fun there must have been at Boulters one day in May 1893 when the *My Queen* from Hampton Court passed through with passengers from the boards of the music hall who jumped out (in fact, one of them jumped *in* by mistake) and entertained the lock-loungers with dance and song.

The *Advertiser* waxed wrathful, too, when members of Ye Lion Slate Club from Henley appeared on the *River Queen* one weekday in 1900, when the sons of toil should by rights have been increasing the horniness of their already horny hands, leaving such gallivanting to the leisured classes. 'A Saturday excursion', readers were assured, 'would have been more *apropos* for such a party.' In 1898 a beanfeast party passing through Boulters in the *My Queen* were very musical and entertained the lock-loungers with the tragic story of how 'they sat upon the baby on the shore—a thing they had never done before' and with the mysteries connected with 'a little bit of string'.

Cabdrivers—rivalries, fisticuffs and strong language for the moment forgotten—sometimes enjoyed themselves on launch trips. In 1895, in excellent weather, and with the Anglo-Roman band making music on board, a number of cabbies steamed upstream from Maidenhead to Henley, an excursion made possible by the generosity of Maidenhead residents. A similar excursion took place aboard the *Emperor* the following year. The group was photographed in Boulters before setting off; and in the Red Lion meadow at Henley their limbs were exercised in sports, while aboard their lungs were exercised as they lustily bawled songs such as "E ain't a-going to tell', startling browsing cattle in riverside meadows and meditative souls eyeing the rippling stream from erstwhile peaceful spots on the towing path. In 1897 their river trip ended with a singsong at the Greyhound in Maidenhead, disturbing, who knows, the sad-eyed ghost of Charles I who two and a half centuries earlier had met his children there, when the scaffold was already throwing its long shadow over his failed, pathetic days.

Great Western Railway Servants, as they were then called, also favoured the Thames for their outings. In 1884 a party of men from the Parcels Department of the Railway Clearing House took a trip from Taplow to Marlow, where they played cricket and enjoyed a 'sumptuous repast' at a local hostelry, another Greyhound. They went home by special saloon, stepping from under the station's canopy with its fringe of ornamental woodwork into the Dickensian carriages of the Marlow Donkey behind its busily puffing small engine. The Railway's Temperance Union held its annual fête at Maidenhead in 1887 in a meadow opposite Skindles.

Sometimes firms gave their staff an annual outing in the form of a river trip. Workers from the High Wycombe chair-making industry (who during the football season used to appear at Marlow wearing miniature chairs in their hats and support their own team with such fervour that residents in the High Street thought it wise to put up their shutters) had a long day on the *Queen of the Thames*. Higher upstream, a firm's instrument hands had their annual dinner at the Shillingford Bridge Hotel. They had gone by rail to Oxford where they embarked in the *Fashion*, lunching on board at Iffley lock, and returning home from Reading. A party from the linoleum works at Staines had a jollification on the *My Queen*, and a large party of compositors from Windsor and district on the *Kestrel*. Employees of a Maidenhead ironmon-

PLATE 19 Yachts racing at Bourne End

PLATE 20 One of the rare quiet days at Boulters for Turner and his companion

PLATE 21 Fishing from a punt moored in mid-stream, with tents on the bank in the background: an idyllic summer scene (*Photo: Frith & Co*)

PLATE 22 In the upper reaches: placing grig weels in position

ger went to Chertsey on the *Mayflower* with a string band on
board, and those of a builder to Sonning with similar musical
accompaniment, their band playing 'Auld Lang Syne' when
home was reached. London cabinet makers and upholsterers
invaded Cookham, about a hundred employees of a London
wholesale saddlers and ironmongers descended on Maidenhead, while in 1897 the staff of a Wealdstone photographic
materials company were on the Thames recording the scene
on their Kodaks. Various working men's institutes hired
steamers for excursions, and children from London or from
schools or workhouses in riverside towns were treated to
similar trips.

Sometimes a household's servants were given a day's
outing on the river. Social mirth and harmony prevailed on
board the *Gainsborough* when one such party had their annual
excursion from Taplow to Henley in 1893, their day too
ending with 'Auld Lang Syne' and also the National Anthem.
In 1885 Sir Roger Palmer, a veteran of the Charge of the
Light Brigade who lived on Glen Island near Boulters,
treated his servants and their friends to an outing to
Medmenham Abbey in his own steam launch. The butler and
housekeeper were directed to see that nothing was wanting
and to make the day as enjoyable as possible. A 'substantial
luncheon' was partaken of; later there was supper and
dancing for several hours. After the butler had proposed a
vote of thanks to Sir Roger and Lady Palmer, the proceedings
were brought to an end in the usual patriotic fashion.

In late Victorian times the Early Closing Movement sprang
up. Its object was to establish a new custom whereby shops
were to shut one afternoon a week. Pale-cheeked drapers'
assistants—weary from long hours of standing and heaving
heavy bolts of material from shelf to counter—were to close
the doors of their emporia and breathe the sweet air of heaven,
and grocers were to put up their shutters on the mingled smell
of cheese, bacon, coffee and firelighters and draw into their
lungs the scent of flowers and the fragrance of newly cut grass.
In 1886 the Windsor and Eton Early Closing Association
went by steam launch to Cliveden where they danced on the
lawn; and in 1888 and 1889 the Maidenhead Association also

took steamer trips in the *Mayflower*, disporting themselves on
the lawn of the Compleat Angler and singing as they slid
along the stream's glassy surface. In 1891 Reading Ironmongers embarked for the Bull at Streatley on board the *Chic* to
celebrate the 2 o'clock Early Closing Movement and on
arrival did full justice to an excellent repast.

Military parties, too, took river trips. The Berkshire
Yeomanry were out in the *Chic*. Guards from the Windsor
barracks enjoyed excursions; colonial soldiers, in England for
Queen Victoria's Diamond Jubilee celebrations in 1897,
steamed in the *Mayflower* from Richmond to Windsor, where
they were entertained at the Horse Guards barracks, and the
following day continued to Caversham and visited the
barracks there. Two launches laden with officers and men of
the 1st Grenadiers passed through Boulters in 1893, all save
the officers and the band clad in white jackets. The band
played as the launches slowly floated up past the green slime
of the lock walls.

Various church groups and choirs hired steamers, singing
solos, duets, quartettes, choruses and glees as they glided
along. A Maidenhead church choir were on the river in 1880,
and 'the excursion was enlivened by some very good choral
singing . . . and after tea an hour was devoted to some secular
pieces of the better sort which were capitally rendered'. One
church party was amused by an Italian boy with an accordian
who turned somersaults and played popular airs, and invited
him on board their steamer. He left: 'with his pockets well-
lined with coppers. Even clergymen seem to admire Miss
Lottie Collins's song, for in response to the clerical request the
dark-skinned youngster tipped off "Ta-ra-ra-boom-de-ay".'

Members of the Salvation Army used the river to spread
their message, and in 1888 the 'naval brigade', numbering
about twenty-five, from their Clapton training homes, arrived by steamer in Maidenhead under the command of Miss
Lucy Booth. These 'lady tars', wearing dark blue bodices
with sailor collars and appearing odd to contemporary eyes on
account of their bustle-less and steel-less skirts, proceeded to
the town hall where songs were sung and speeches made amid
a veritable hail of 'Amen's, 'Hallelujah!'s and 'Praise the

Lord!'s, after which some were billeted in the town, while others steamed off to Marlow in a downpour.

A group of Freemasons on the *Queen of the Thames* had an unfortunate experience, for on arrival at Medmenham they were for some reason 'denied the Englishman's usual privilege—a drink!' They re-embarked expressing their displeasure by the strains of 'Poor Cock Robin' and the 'Dead March' in *Saul* and consoled themselves with a 'substantial meat tea' at the Great Western Hotel at Reading before returning to London by train.

No such misfortunes overtook the Maidenhead Licensed Victuallers Protection Association who took good care to ensure a plentiful supply of both victuals and those fluids for which a licence was required when they set out on such trips. In 1896, when they steamed upstream under a sunny sky for their twenty-third annual excursion, after throwing coppers to mudlarks who ran alongside for about two miles near Marlow, they adjourned for luncheon—consisting of salmon, chicken, duck, lamb, beef, ham, cucumber, lettuce, potatoes, beans, marrows, plum tart, apple tart, blancmange, cheese etc (the mind boggles to imagine what the 'etc' might have covered)—which was followed by a fine spread at teatime.

The Maidenhead Volunteer Fire Brigade also made river excursions from time to time. In the autumn of 1880 they embarked upstream in Bond's new electric steamer *Formosa*, flag flying, quadrille band playing, and here and there a touch of russet on the Cliveden and Quarry Woods marking the onset of the year's decay. After a hearty luncheon on the lawn of the Medmenham Abbey Hotel, under the elms, they presented 'an elegantly-braided full dress tunic' to their captain, than whom 'a more worthy man it would be impossible to find'. They insisted he put it on; the band, amid cheers, played 'Auld Lang Syne'; and there was in due course a knife and fork tea. The *Formosa* had 'an ample supply of fluids' on board.

From time to time a wedding party travelled by river. One such party was very musical in Boulters in 1891; and in 1907 when 'a well-known river habitué' married, one steam and five electric launches decorated in green and white glided to

Bray church, the bridesmaids in a bower of cherry blossom, liliums, spirea, palms, ferns and other plants. Some wore white and some pale mauve, and all carried bouquets of pink roses. Hundreds assembled on the banks to watch this lovely spectacle.

River excursions were by no means confined to the lower and middle classes. As early as 1875 'a somewhat fashionable and numerously attended picnic' travelled by pleasure barge from Maidenhead to Marlow to dine at the Crown. Launches were hired by many distinguished people. In 1908 Andrews of Maidenhead, in response to a royal command received by telegram, prepared his electric launch *The Angler* for the use of Queen Alexandra and other members of the royal family, who travelled from the royal landing stage at Windsor upstream to Cookham and back. A Japanese prince and princess, the Japanese ambassador and members of the embassy staff hired the *Flosshilde* and the *Empress of India* in 1909; it was said that when the little princess first saw her launch and its decorations she clapped her hands with delight. Other foreign visitors were shown the beauties of the Thames from the decks of steamers. They included a party of Indian princes—whose native costume 'attracted no little attention'—and a Chinese prince, also in native costume, who was a cause of merriment to young lock-loungers at Boulters who had not yet achieved the age of politeness, for they appeared highly amused at 'the celestial's pig-tail'.

In 1905, amid scenes of tremendous enthusiasm, a group of officers of the French fleet and their ladies set off from Maidenhead for Cookham in nine electric launches. Bystanders waved hats and handkerchiefs as they embarked from Skindles' landing stage to the strains of the Marseillaise. Occupants of boats stood up and waved their hats. Those at tea waved their cups. A local resident made a speech of welcome in French; the uncomprehending crowd seized the occasion to applaud every time he paused for breath; and the French officers, who all took off their hats and bowed as he left, moved out of Boulters to the sound of 'crashing hurrahs'.

The Prowse Agency organised river trips, conveying thirty-five or more 'Arries and 'Arriets by third-class compartment from Paddington to Windsor and taking them for a day on the river, with lunch, dinner and tea provided, all for 14s a head. Clients paying a guinea a head could travel by private saloon from London to Reading, take a launch trip to Maidenhead, consume similar but more elaborate meals, and return to London from Taplow. The cheap menus were advertised in English, but on the most expensive ones even simple items appeared in French. Hampers also could be delivered to London addresses or railway termini, and waiters hired for 12s 6d a day plus expenses. For just under £11, a dozen people could picnic luxuriously on mayonnaise of salmon, four roast chicken, a forequarter of lamb, a pigeon, veal and ham or steak pie, a tongue, three lobsters, salad, rolls, bread, cheese, biscuits, eight bottles of champagne, two of sherry, two of claret, one of brandy, one of whisky, and eighteen of seltzer or soda water. A block of ice was also provided.

Salters, the Oxford boat firm, ran regular steamer trips from that city to Kingston; and although this service was at one point stopped because it was unprofitable, it had been revived by 1888, and in 1891 the *Lock to Lock Times* commented: 'Salters' Thames trip has now become really famous. Scarcely a week has passed lately without one or other of the illustrated journals coming out with pictorial accounts of the voyage.' The return fare was 25s about that time, exclusive of food and overnight accommodation en route. The Lamb at Wallingford catered for Salters parties, providing luncheon for half-a-crown; and light refreshments were available on the boat. As G. D. Leslie wrote:

> The passengers on board are chiefly composed of a class of people who would not otherwise see the river in any way; quiet, middle-aged townsfolk, many of them, perhaps, taking the trip on their only holiday, mixed with a few old ladies and invalids, who may be deterred by nervousness from other river excursions, form the bulk of the passengers.

Of all those, high or low, aristocratic or vulgar, who watched brown waters, green meadows and trailing willows slide by as they sat ensconced on the deck of a Thames steamer, no more pathetic party was carried than that

described by the *Lock to Lock Times* as embarking on the
Snowdrop one summer day in 1890. These were the inmates
of Richmond workhouse:

> . . . the poor old women flickered up into a transient gaiety and
> danced a little on deck; the men smoked their pipes . . . the ruling
> spirit of the event the Rev. Astley Cooper, and the Master and
> other officials, exerted themselves in their care for the comfort
> and pleasure of the 'guests'.

At a concert that evening, recollecting the beauties of the
day, they listened to 'Sweet Dreamland Faces' and 'The
Better Land'.

> How many a face must have started out of the shadows of the
> past—how many a thought must have run forward towards that
> better land—as those poor bankrupts sat there—each with a past,
> and all with a future—beyond the workhouse walls! . . . 'In-
> asmuch as ye did it unto them, ye did it unto Me.'

There followed a list of the contributors to the day's
expenses.

19

LAUNCHES AND ADIPOSE STOCKBROKERING-LOOKING BIPEDS

Many launches were coal powered. For their owners, these 'tea kettles' as they were once described had certain disadvantages. They vibrated; the coal created dirt (a steamer going through Marlow lock produced a cloud of smuts spoiling ladies' dresses) and took up space on board. Great heat and a smell of oil were sent out from their engine rooms. Electric launches, which vibrated hardly at all, were clean, quiet and tended to make less wash, became very popular, and Dickens described them in the early 1890s as bidding fair shortly to supersede steamers. About this time Mr Pears of the soap firm acquired a new launch, the *Glow-worm*, built of bright mahogany with teak fittings, lit as well as propelled by electricity, carrying a search light, and capable of taking forty passengers. The electric *Golden Grasshopper*, with white awning and hangings, and plum coloured cushions, appeared at Marlow regatta in 1889; it seems to have had some connection with the houseboat of the same name mentioned in Chapter 12. Those on board and all connected with it wore brooches and pins in the form of grasshoppers. When Turner first went to Boulters, electric launches were not thought of, but by 1898 there were hundreds. They were pioneered by the firm of Immisch, were included in the fleets offered for hire by boat-builders, and exported to Venice and Bolivia.

But for all their popularity, electric launches suffered from one great drawback. They could not travel more than about thirty miles without being re-charged, delaying their passengers each time for some few hours. There were charging stations (mostly barges or tugs fitted with engines and complete electrical plant) at Hampton, Weybridge, Chertsey,

Bray, Marlow, Henley, Reading, Shillingford and Oxford. At
Maidenhead a number of boat-builders provided this service.
People hiring these launches for a few hours only did not
suffer any inconvenience, as they all carried enough electricity for one day's running. However, electric launches—from
a small one called *Multum in Parvo* to the large excursion
vessels hired by boat-builders—failed to hold their own
against steamers. By 1907 the latter had improved in construction and ran more quietly: in any case, as J. E. Vincent
complained in *The Story of the Thames*, not long afterwards:
'in this age of gramophones, the worst noises seem to be
tolerated in a wonderful way'.

Naphtha-powered motors for launches were an innovation
of the 1880s. They weighed only 200lb apiece, cost 9d to 10d
an hour to run and, like electricity, saved space, had the
advantages of cleanliness, and diminished vibration and the
amount of wash created. Naphtha-powered launches could
be stopped in their own length when going at speed, and
turned in a very small circle, but they too had their drawback,
for the stench they made lingered in locks and even got into
the clothes of people following in small boats. The editor of
the *Lock to Lock Times* (the 'Eddy-tor' as he facetiously wrote
himself) complained of it, and his magazine said of the
naphtha launch *The Torment*: 'how appropriately named!'
Regulations introduced about 1904 forbade these vessels to
'lock' with small boats.

This rule applied also to petrol-powered launches, which
Vincent described as growing in popularity in the early years
of the twentieth century. Edward VII had acquired one by
1903, and 547 were registered in 1912. The Thames Conservancy was alive to the dangerous nature of these vessels,
and arranged for bins of sand to be placed at each lock below
Oxford in case the oil or spirit used in them caused fire; but
despite the precautions taken there was an occasional accident. The lock-keeper at Mapledurham was presented with
two guineas and an address of congratulation by Lord
Desborough in his capacity as chairman of the Conservancy,
for extinguishing a fire on board a motor launch at great
personal risk. After Maidenhead regatta in 1912 one such

launch was gutted by fire after an explosion. The passengers got off safely, as did the engineer, though with badly scorched face and eyes; cushions and other inflammable items were thrown overboard, the fire extinguished with soil from the bank, and the St John's Ambulance people on duty had a lively day coping with this emergency as well as staunching the seven wounds suffered by the young victim of a severe case of dog bite. Although by 1913 bylaws had reduced the risk of fire, a more serious accident took place at Hurley the following year, when the force of an explosion on board a motor launch blew the engineer and another man into the river. Both required treatment for burns, and the engineer lost a finger, but the other occupants of the launch managed to get it to the bank and escape before it sank.

One winter Sunday in 1881, Mr G. H. Vansittart of Bisham Abbey walked down the path of the small grey church which stood neighbour on the river bank to his ancestral acres. Passing lofty elms and mellowed brickwork, smelling as he went the cold, sweet air of the morning fresh against his face, he entered a nearby meadow. Then an unexpected noise mingled with the ringing biblical phrases still sounding in his ears, and turning he saw two steamers speeding along the river. Their wash curled over the Buckinghamshire towing path, carrying away lumps of soil and, by the other bank, lifting a moored boat on the crest of high waves.

Speeding was only one of the crimes committed by steam launches, which even thus early, the year after the first steamer actually built on the Upper Thames was launched from the yard of Messrs Horsham at Bourne End, were beginning to create as much bitterness on the river as motor cars were later to create on its banks. Launches hired by excursionists were sometimes delayed at locks, after which they speeded in an effort to regain lost time. On one occasion a loud bang resounded over the water and water meadows below Temple Mills, as the *Empress of India* and the *Bona Fide* crashed into each other, one having parts of her bows knocked off and the other being holed in the side.

A steamboat had passed by Reading for the first time as early as 1813, and thirty years later the passenger steamer

Locomotive had caused £300 worth of damage to towing paths
and other works between Teddington and Hampton Court,
Thames Ditton residents complaining that the wash was
undermining their lawns and meadows. Complaints about
launches from other river-users rose to a crescendo towards
the end of the century. Walter Armstrong tracked some of
these dragons to their lair, and wrote in *The Thames from its
Rise to the Nore* of 1889:

> Just before getting to Chiswick, we are startled by a row of
> corrugated iron sheds on the north bank, which with the lazy
> leisure of our journey from Lechlade behind us, come like a
> foretaste of some rest-annihilating pandemonium. These sheds
> are Thorneycroft's yard for the building of steam launches, more
> especially of the murderous kind known as torpedo boats. From
> morning till night the din of hammers and of every conceivable
> weapon for the destruction of peace rings from these hideous
> roofs.

About this time a lady sculler wrote from Marlow to the
Lock to Lock Times complaining of the reckless steering of a
steam launch which had forced her to ship a scull very quickly
to prevent it from being broken. After it had passed, 'the
gentleman (?) steering her looked back at us and simply
grinned in a most aggravating manner'. The 'gentleman (?)'
gave further proof of the turpitude of his character in the
magazine's next edition, writing to say that he had in fact been
smiling sympathetically, wondering if he should go to help
'these amateur skiff-women'.

Launches were meant to give way to smaller boats, but
rarely did so. The wash of speeding launches, as well as
damaging banks and soaking people and cushions in little
boats, could dislodge spawn and sometimes lifted small fry
out of the water, leaving them to die a gasping death.
Sometimes these unpopular vessels were noisy: not only did
rowdy songs and loud rude remarks emanate from launch-
loads of 'Arries in an advanced state of intoxication, but a
correspondent was writing to the *Maidenhead Advertiser*
from Marlow in 1880:

> 'Nature's sweet restorer, balmy sleep' for those residents who
> may have unfortunately taken up what they once believed to be a

calm and peaceful abode in the neighbourhood of the river is now
only a dream of the past, in consequence of the belching forth by
certain steam launches of sounds so hideous as to make Sunday
and weekday in the vicinity unbearable, which may be extremely
funny to the owners but is only evidence of their extreme
vulgarity.

The *Lock to Lock Times* reported that the devotions of the
congregations during church services at Staines in 1888 were
disturbed by a fog signal, a 'horrible instrument of mental
torture', being tried out by its owner. A couple of years later
the whistle of a launch at Marlow could be heard for miles,
and in 1895 the owner of the luxurious *Flying Fish* was up
before the bench at Maidenhead summoned for causing her
whistle to be used to the annoyance of the public. Asked if he
was guilty, he replied: 'Well, I really can't say. I can't write
down every time I blow the whistle.' The temptation to use it
must have been overwhelming: the noise it made was rather
like a bomb exploding. The owner was fined, and before the
end of the century the Thames Conservancy issued its notice
to control the whistling of launches and tugs.

Other court cases dealt with accidents and damage caused
by launches. Spencer Brunton, gentleman, was prosecuted
for speeding as early as 1876. *Elsa* was said to have rushed at
over 10mph in 1879, and this led to a £2 fine. The captain of
the *Queen of the Thames* suffered a penalty of only £5 when he
ran down a punt and immersed its occupants during the
firework display after Bourne End regatta in 1904. 'You
might as well call out to the Flying Dutchman', declared a
witness at a court case following an incident in which a
speeding launch hit a fishing punt moored to a ryepeck so that
one of its occupants was knocked off his chair and but for the
ryepeck would have been immersed. While the Maidenhead
Licensed Victuallers warded off starvation during their
outing in 1880, *Wild Rose*, *Undine* and *Formosa*, on which
they were attending to this important matter, raced at Hurley.
Doubtless, said the defence at the subsequent court case, they
had been trying to make up for lost time as they had been
warned that Cookham lock was under repair.

Sometimes there were scenes at locks. A steamer navigated

without due care and caution coming out of Cookham lock, hurried against another in front and broke her flagstaff. The navigator did not care to have his fault pointed out, and used abusive language when told to pull up and see what damage he had done. Turner occasionally had to deal with awkward customers and sometimes there were fines for disobeying his orders. He refused to pass Sir Richard Mansell's launch without adequate lights, whereupon that gentleman went to the wheel on the lock bridge and began to raise the sluices, having 'd——d the lock-keeper and the lights too', and declared that Turner was a skunk. Another launch rushed into Boulters not giving boats a chance to get out, and the *Nip-Nip* was fined for being 'too nippy' and going into Boulters before the *Humble Bee* and others, against Turner's orders.

From time to time there was a serious accident, as when in 1911 the *May Queen* ran down a skiff between Hampton Court and Richmond. The Thames Conservancy (prosecuting) alleged that her captain was drunk and he was fined the full penalty which at that time was only £20. His victims had survived by clinging to the launch until they could be hauled on board. Amazing discrepancies were to be found in the evidence given by witnesses when speeding cases came up in court. The complainants, their friends, and anyone who had seen the accident and loathed launches, invariably swore that shocking speeds had been achieved by these 'voracious jacks' and 'river sharks'. All the occupants of the launch, on the other hand, were only too ready to hurry forward to claim that the vessel had been travelling so slowly that the only possible conclusion was that her mechanism was at fault. In 1884, for example, the occupant of a rowing boat stated that he had been borne down by a steam launch which if he had not altered his course would have cut him in two. She was travelling, he said, at 8 to 10mph. But the court also heard that she was creeping along at only 1mph, sounding her whistle continuously; and as this latter speed was confirmed by some watermen who had seen the incident, the case was dismissed.

A sculler wrote to the *Lock to Lock Times* complaining about a launch on the wrong side of the river:

... my boat was kept in the centre ... On seeing me in that position the man with the rudder yawed over to the towing-path side, and the assumed owner, an adipose stockbrokering-looking biped, armed with fat legs and the usual City impedimenta above, howled out to me to 'pull 'ard' and get out of his way ... The usual beer bottles, dirty champagne cases and other drinking debris appertaining to your obese City gent, were of course displayed with ostentatious vulgarity.

'Christmas Eve with Father Thames', the doggerel verses appearing in the *Lock to Lock Times* of 1888, featured the steam launch owner under the heading 'The Bloated Oofocrat sings' and showed that venerable gentleman reprimanding him. A cartoon by Fred Walker which appeared in *Punch* under the title of 'Captain Jinks of the *Selfish*' showed a number of bloated oofocrats sitting smoking in easy, debonair attitudes, facing inward and ignoring the scenery, in a speeding steamer which took no account of other river users. A sculler, tossed on her wash, was losing his sculls, an artist (representing G. D. Leslie) painting on the river was sent flying, and a fisherman looked anxiously at the wash. Copies were sent to the launch's proprietor, and the likeness of the captain was so good that he was easily recognised by river people; but alas, the nuisance continued unabated.

Leslie explained that passengers generally sat with their backs to the view as, in the bows, wind and spray rendered 'a steady gaze a-head very uncomfortable and a smoke out of the question', while in the stern the launch's smoke and swell spoilt the view. Everything aboard was gritty and black and these drawbacks, combined with vibration, the stench of engine oil and the stuffiness of the cabin, forced him to the conclusion that pride of possession was the real motive for owning a steamer:

> ... the pride of being seen as the captain of a private yacht adorned with brass nobs [sic] and polished fittings, brass-banded water-casks, gilding, monograms, flags etc; to go puffing along with a stoker and boy under your command; the pleasure of whistling to announce yourself to the lock-keepers, or to warn boats in front; to have an excuse for wearing the manly flannels of the rowing man, without exercising a single muscle in them.

Mr Bickerdyke, fertile of ideas, information and indignation, fulminated against the steamer, 'the terror of the
Thames'. He suggested the time had come to revert to the old
horse-drawn pleasure barges—'broad, safe, beamy affairs,
with a cabin below and a deck above'—and put down the
trouble caused by steamers to the fact that they were built by
skiff builders who did not know the lines suitable for their
construction. In 1870, he pointed out, there were only 6 of
'these pests', but by the mid 1890s there were about 400,
about one every quarter of a mile. He considered that
navigators should be licensed like cabbies, risking the loss of
their licences for travelling dangerously, and took the
Thames Conservancy to task for tending to act against
launches only if there was an accident.

With so much enmity to contend with, steam-launch
owners formed a protection society, receiving the encourage-
ment of the Prince of Wales and of Vicat Cole whose pictures
of the upper reaches, despite the presence of launches there,
breathe the very spirit of peace. One owner feared that if they
did not unite to protect themselves steamers would be driven
off the river. Even the *Maidenhead Advertiser* expressed a
certain sympathy with the steersman:

> If he only splash a puntsman, or rock the craft of a fond couple
> under Cliveden woods, all the terrors of a Conservancy pro-
> secution forthwith descend upon his devoted head, and a
> substantial fine, accompanied by fierce adjuration, is the lightest
> penalty that can befall him.

In 1882 the Thames Launch Owners' Association held its
first annual meeting in London and by the following year
could inform its members that the frivolous prosecutions
which were once frequent had ceased.

The majority of launch owners and navigators, it seems,
did abide by the laws of courtesy. A letter from Maidenhead
appearing in the *Daily Express* in 1913 complained of the
speed and 'reckless blackguardism' of the rich 'river hogs'
driving motor and electric launches—offenders who were
always the same, whom the Thames Conservancy officials
knew well, but would not punish until someone, probably a

'comparatively inexpert girl', was thrown out of a punt and drowned. The following edition of the *Maidenhead Advertiser* described this letter as grossly exaggerated.

Dream Faces was seen on the river in 1892 with no one at the wheel. Appropriately her flag was a skull and crossbones and an hour glass. All the passengers were the worse for drink, the man in charge was intoxicated in the engine room and 'not in his proper senses; he was sort of happy go lucky', the engineer was lying on his stomach, and the launch proceeded in zigzag fashion down Cookham lock cut. If the rich river hog was often drunk with his own importance, this was not always perhaps the most dangerous form of intoxication.

20

LESSER BOATS AND BARGES

Lesser boats had less power to make trouble, but sometimes stretched that power to its limits. A man in a rowing boat and in charge of two others refused to move at Boulters when asked to do so at a busy time, assaulted the occupant of another vessel, and put his boathook through the side of a new mahogany skiff. When asked by a policeman to give his name and address, he replied: 'I have no name or address, and come from nowhere.'

Amateurs afloat were the cause of many a headache to the long-suffering lock-keeper and the experienced river man, and sometimes the cause of a wan smile. 'Mind your right *thing*', said a man attempting to steer, at Henley regatta in 1888. 'Turn to the right. Go round the corner.' Sometimes steerers failed to 'go round the corner' as they should have done, and one such error in 1893 led to a real-life replica of the collision described a few years before by Jerome K. Jerome in which the three men in a boat, instead of sailing into the realm of twilight, sailed into a fishing punt moored in mid-stream. The *Maidenhead Advertiser* reported: 'When the collision occurred, the three anglers with one accord cried "——!!" And when they had regained their footing they demanded, with one voice, "Where the —— are you coming to?" ' a *Punch* cartoon showed the victim of a collision clinging to his boat which floated upside down. 'I'm sorry, sir, but it was your own fault', said the party responsible. 'Why didn't you get out into mid-stream?' 'Why,' came the plaintive retort, 'that's just what I've done!'

The amateur brandishing his boathook, endangering everything in sight from freshly varnished boats to human flesh, was a character sufficiently dreaded by other river-users to earn the sobriquet 'the boathook fiend'. A series of cartoons in a *Lock to Lock Times* of 1888 related his life history, from

PLATE 23 Streatley Mill, showing 'brethren of the brush' (*The Royal River*)

PLATE 24 'The Boating Season: "In Tow"' (*Illustrated London News*, 1899)

PLATE 25 'Rival Attractions: Pedal or Paddle' (*Illustrated London News*, 1898)

dreadful infancy during which 'a fiendish light would flash in his eyes if he could only smash his feeding bottle and secure a piece of broken glass with which he could scrape the paint off the furniture' to his death when 'he was taken to where he ought always to have been' by the Devil about to thrust him into the eternal flames.

Cumbersome old tubs were rowed in the early years of the nineteenth century. In the 1830s sides were lowered. In due course outriggers came in, then keel-less boats, then sliding seats which were introduced, with swivel rowlocks, at Henley regatta in 1879. H. R. Robertson enumerated and described the boats used by pleasure-seekers on the Thames in the mid 1870s: punts, dinghies, rowing boats (pair-oared gigs, later superseded by skiffs), randans, funnies and whiffs. The randan was crewed by a sculler sitting between two rowers, and was sufficiently roomy to take several passengers; in later years, it appears, triple sculling was the custom. A funny too was sculled. It was outrigged, with stem and stern alike, the keel falling away in a sloping curve from either end. A whiff was similar, but with upright stern. By 1878 Canadian canoes from Ontario were appearing on the Thames (one was advertised in a *Lock to Lock Times* of 1891 as having mast and sail, velvet-pile cushions, cane backboards and Brussels carpet), but by 1908 they had had their day. Rob Roy canoes were all the rage when Turner went to Boulters in 1880, and there were then only three private launches one of which belonged to Sir Roger Palmer, who still owned it twenty-four years later.

Punts were originally regarded primarily as fishing craft, but about 1880 narrow mahogany ones fitted for sailing were much seen below Henley, and punts were the most popular boats of the early 1900s. Ladies had made the art of punting particularly their own since Abel Beesley, the professional champion, had introduced a less laborious method of propelling these craft. In 1906 punt cushions to suit the river were described as the latest fashion for the enthusiastic river girl. Covers were cool green for hot days, scarlet for grey days, and pale blue 'under the silvery rays of the moon', and there were different covers for different hours of the day. Ladies, reported the *Morning Post* in 1911, were taking so large a part in the life of the river that they had changed its character; their influence too was noticeable in the adornment of bungalows and houseboats.

Picnics on banks and islands had been a conspicuous feature of earlier years, but because of the rubbish left behind certain riparian owners had by this time ceased to allow the public to invade their properties. Hampers were now taken on punts, and people had their meals on adjustable tables on board. The popularity of punting with the sterner sex, too, was noted. Formerly the river man was a rowing man, sharing a double-sculling punt with two or three friends with whom he would take turns at pulling and steering, proud of the correctness of his form. By 1912 a three-mile pull was generally considered to be quite enough, and the disappearance of long-distance rowing at the rate of ten or fifteen miles a morning was held up by some as a sign of the decay of British athleticism. Such people probably regarded with horror the appearance of the motor canoe about this time. This was made of mahogany, with an electric engine placed low down to make it as steady as a punt. In 1912 there were only two in the neighbourhood of Maidenhead; by 1914 there were many, their increased popularity among the wealthy being a feature of the season. But those who looked askance at such effortless boating chose a strange year to lament the decline of British manhood!

In the mid 1870s the best class rowing boats cost about 25s per foot. By late Victorian days the best quality randan skiff cost about £40 fully equipped. Eights averaged £60, fours £35, pairs £22, scullers' boats for racing (including oars and sliding seats) £15. A pair-oared skiff with tent cover, movable seats, and mattress could be hired for £3 15s a week in 1883. On fine summer Sundays a busy trade in letting boats for the day was carried on at up-river resorts. As much as 50s could be made on a single craft at Maidenhead in 1899. Double was usually paid on Ascot Sunday, and sometimes more, yet on that day in 1913 Bonds, the Maidenhead boat firm, let their fleet of thirty launches and a hundred punts and skiffs, and had to hire from elsewhere.

Bad weather during the Henley regatta of 1907 spelt disaster for small firms hoping to let boats there. Thousands of these craft had converged on the town, arriving by road or river at the cost of about 30s each. Firms hired plots for regatta week which were auctioned just before for about £15 each, and demand was particularly keen for those by the station where customers could be caught as soon as they arrived and boats hired to them for £2 a day (or £3 for the final day) in a good year. But in 1907 hirers were pleased to get 10s, and some who had taken fifty craft were quite unable to let them. The bigger firms suffered less as they generally let in advance and were paid whether their boats were used or not; also they let many for the season.

A Maidenhead resident who died in the late 1880s remembered a time when only one boat could be hired between Maidenhead bridge and Boulters, and in the 1860s only six were available. A local fisherman offered a boat for hire at Shepperton in 1846, and at Windsor too about that time one man had pleasure boats for hire, and another let them out to Eton boys. The splendour of watermen's uniform on that part of the river made up for the comparative modesty of the boat business, for a photograph of about 1850 shows a top-hatted waterman resplendent in a frock-coat with epaulettes and gilt or silver-gilt buttons down the front and on the sleeves. By 1880 this uniform was replaced by a beribboned straw hat, white breeches, and a many-buttoned jacket. In 1902 most of Immisch's boatmen were uniformed.

Boats could be hired from Salters, and when they were finished with left with watermen who would undertake to look after them for half-a-crown apiece until the firm, notified by postcard, sent to collect them. Leslie noted: 'boat-vans pass my door at Remenham pretty nearly every day in July and August, with five or six boats to a load, and are the great delight of my children'. Salters had agents at landing places, and they were among those firms which could equip camping parties with everything they needed, including neatly packed hampers of crockery.

Among their customers were the Pennells, who set out one rainy morning from Salters' boathouse in a pair-oared skiff—

a tent-boat of the type so warmly recommended by that useful publication *Pearson's Gossipy Guide to the Thames from Source to Sea*. At night they stretched the waterproof cover over iron hoops, prepared their meal with the aid of Salters' 'ingenious stove with kettles and frying-pans fitting into each-other like the pieces of a Chinese puzzle', then fell asleep under a 'long green tunnel'. Mrs Pennell had never before steered, her husband had scarcely ever rowed a boat, they had not the least idea how to manage it, and neither could swim. Notwithstanding all these handicaps, they saw the next day dawn 'suffused with that soft shrouding mist you see nowhere but England', and survived to write of their month's excursion in *The Stream of Pleasure*. Their compatriot Mr Wellington Wack travelled in the *Fuzzy Wuzzy*:

> . . . a light, tippy, fifteen-foot canoe, prettily ribbed with ash and cedar, and decked-in fourteen inches from stern and bow . . . A sturdy boy could lug her over a portage of five hundred yards. She could, and did, spill out her cargo on so slight a favour as the shifting of my pipe from the windward to the leeward side.

The best punts, said Leslie, were built at Maidenhead, the worst further downstream, those built at Surbiton being beautifully finished in their workmanship, but detestable for shoving purposes. His own, built by Woodhouse of Bray, was 'a beauty', her sides two long slabs of mahogany, with no join in them, and all her screws of brass. Fred Walker the artist had a small, light punt which 'from the thinness of its skin and general shakiness was nicknamed *The Strawberry Pottle*'; and James Englefield, 'Red Quill' of *The Field* and author of *The Delightful Life of Pleasure on the Thames*, also had a light-weight one built at Eton which served him for thirty years. In 1891 F. O. Wethered, captain of the Marlow Rowing Club, had a 'wonderful punt' built for him, very long but only 1ft wide, with a large parallel piece of bamboo fixed about 3ft away by means of cross-pieces of bamboo. This floated on the water to prevent him upsetting.

Three enterprising ladies calling themselves 'The Three Queries' turned a punt into a floating tea shop in 1908, even supplying 'tea baskets' containing ample for a meal, at a very reasonable price. That same summer, a punt with a piano in the bows drew up at Skindles where, from beneath rows of Chinese lanterns, visitors were entertained by a Verdi duet. A punt called *The Absent-Minded Beggar* (a quotation from Kipling) featured on the float of Wilder's, the local boat-building firm, in a procession through Maidenhead at the time of the South African War. A member of the family was L. Wilder, a professional fisherman and, like Sir Roger Palmer, a Crimean veteran, and on the punt under a brilliant canopy of Japanese lanterns stood one of his young relations clad in khaki, carrying a toy rifle, the Balaclava medals proudly displayed on his chest.

More unusual boats made their appearance from time to time. Taunt lived for a while in a flat-bottomed boat moored at Oxford—a 'lotus-eating existence' he called it. Sir Roger Palmer had a large canal boat which he named the *Balaclava*, and General G. Higginson of Marlow, who was known as 'the father of the Grenadiers', used to float by gondola down the backwater leading from his house to the river. Several of these craft were to be seen on the river, especially at regattas, sometimes paddled by Venetian gondoliers. There were dongolas, and at the Reading Amateur regatta of 1888, a dhow and a Maori dugout with scarlet awning crewed by ladies. The dugout also appeared at Henley that year.

Lock tickets for pleasure craft were instituted in 1870 from Penton Hook downwards, but in earlier days certain unofficial charges were sometimes made on the non-tidal Thames, even if these were only in the form of a lock-keeper's hopeful look and half-extended palm. By 1875 owners of the smallest class of boats could buy a day's lock-pass for 3d, or a season ticket for £1; later in the decade the Thames Conservancy were increasing annual payments and tolls for many types of pleasure traffic. Registration came next, with registration plates on all boats. By 1891 Boulters and Molesey locks could bring in as much as £60 in tolls on a good Sunday, and by the end of the century 10,482 pleasure boats were registered.

Barges and tugs, although diminishing in numbers, continued to ply their trade up and down the river, frequently

annoying the occupants of pleasure boats especially when
they wanted to go through locks at the same time during busy
summer weekends. The barge *Sam*, carrying 7,300 gallons of
tar from the Maidenhead gas works to London, sank in Bray
lock in 1890. The *Sarah Ann* was once detained two days at
Boulters owing to the illness of the bargee's wife, which
illness culminated in the appearance on the scene of a 'little
stranger'.

Barges occupying a very different place in the social scale,
formerly corporation state barges or the property of City
companies, were moored along the Oxford river bank from
early Victorian times for use as college lounges and dressing-
rooms. During Eights Week their decks were crowded with
enthusiastic undergraduates, sisters and sweethearts, and
occasionally were the scene of concerts or dances under
Japanese lanterns swinging in the summer breeze. The Oriel
barge retained its delicate form and long sharp prow where
the rowers had sat, bronze figures by the saloon door, and
windows and tarnished gilding. The royal state barge, a
splendid affair, was kept at Teddington. On its gunwales
large brass dolphins curved their tails to form rowlocks; the
figurehead was a mahogany dolphin etched with gold, and the
tiller a brass serpent with ornamental head.

By 1884 the *Maidenhead Advertiser* reported that the
practice of towing small boats on the river was driving out
rowing as far as going against the stream was concerned.
Processions of people towing were to be seen on bank
holidays, a fashion which Richard Jefferies noted and
whimsically described. He saw two gentlemen drawing a
lady; they were clad in:

> ... striped flannels, one streaked with gold, the other with
> scarlet ... They were very earnestly at work, pacing in step, their
> bodies slightly leaning forwards, and every now and then they
> mopped their faces with handkerchiefs which they carried in
> their girdles. Something in their slightly bowed attitude re-
> minded me of the captives depicted on Egyptian monuments,
> with cords about their necks. How curious is that instinct which
> makes each sex, in different ways, the willing slave of the other!
> These human steam-tugs paced and pulled ... An interval, and

still more gentlemen in flannel, labouring like galley-slaves at the tow-rope, hot, perspiring, and happy after their kind, and ladies under parasols, comfortably seated, cool, and happy after their kind.

21

BOAT-BUILDERS AND THEIR TRADE

Many boat-building firms on the non-tidal Thames were founded, flourished and expanded in later Victorian days. Some professional fishermen who did a little boat-building on the side found that minor part of their businesses growing so profitable that they came to devote all their time to it.

Salters, one of four boat-building firms at Oxford in the early 1870s, were expanding their already large business at that date. They built all kinds of craft to order, and proudly announced that they had built the winning boat in the university boat race nine years running. They offered a large selection for hire—an eight-oar costing £5 a week, a canoe 30s—and their vans travelled from Oxford to Wandsworth twice a month or oftener during the summer. The three Salter brothers, all Wesleyan, Liberal teetotallers, and one of them an Oxford councillor and magistrate, co-operated to their mutual benefit with the Great Western Railway which issued combined rail and river tickets, but avoided offending those who felt strongly on the vexed question of the desecration of the Sabbath, for their steamers did not operate on Sundays.

At Binsey, in the 1880s, a whole settlement lived on letting boats at the lock. T. Tims, an Oxford University Boat Club waterman, expanded into a similar business (watermen too could be hired from him) and was one of those who offered boats for hire at Henley regatta. By 1910 the firm, which had developed to become boat-builders to His Majesty, suffered a disastrous season, the penalty of living by an outdoor activity in an unpredictable climate.

Streatley and Goring, noted the *Lock to Lock Times* in 1891, were giving some very plain tokens of a deep-seated determination to come to the front in the matter of boat-building, while near Pangbourne bridge in the early years of the new century, Mitton noted with regret in *The Thames* 'great launch works which are a blot and an eyesore, but it is so seldom we find our ointment without the proverbial fly'. J. Keel, a Caversham angler and captain of the steam launch *Fashion*, had built a boathouse at Tilehurst by 1891 and was prepared to supply the needs of those residents of the west end of Reading who wished to disport themselves on the river. Bona's new steamer was afloat at Caversham, the sun shining onto her windows of ornamental glass, throwing pools of colour within. The genial-faced W. Moss, too, opened a new boathouse, near to the Reading Rowing Club quarters. He was a great smoker: 'To catch him without his favourite weed would be a clever capture indeed; in fact, he is generally supposed to be liable to a heavy penalty if found without it.' He was well known from Folly Bridge to Teddington, president of the Reading Waltonian Angling Society, head water bailiff for the district, and always ready to assist (vocally) at any concert or entertainment for charitable or other purposes. There was to be a huge 'smoker' for the opening of his new boathouse.

A. H. East, too, had recently built a boathouse above Caversham lock, was enlarging both stock and premises (with more waiting and dressing rooms) and now planned to erect villas at the back for the convenience of his customers. He housed, repaired and varnished 'gentlemen's boats', and was well situated for the railway stations. East also organised riverside concerts. The steam launch *Countess* was added to his stock, and the *Lock to Lock Times* reporter noted the flood of people on promenade, balconies and seats in front of East's and the nearby Adams & Gyngell's boathouses . . . 'the lady novelette reader, the lover, the general lounger or sightseer . . . the nursemaid with her charge'. By 1898 East's were turning themselves into a limited company, by which time their business had expanded to Sandhurst and they were opening a depôt on the Seine.

At Henley, Searle's advertised boats for sale or hire: also 'Ladies & Gentlemen's Dressing Rooms. Gentlemen's Boats Housed, Repaired and Varnished'; while Hobbs' enlarged and beautified their premises. Shaw's premises were on the Buckinghamshire bank by Marlow bridge, and by the 1887

season they had erected 'yet another boathouse'. The launch
the *North Star* lay at anchor awaiting hire, and licensed
fishing punts were available, with or without fishermen.
Shaw's were exporting a double scull in-rigger to Venice in
1889 for use on the Grand Junction Canal, while swarthy
gondoliers from that historic waterway paddled the placid
Thames, and its black surface gave back tremulous reflections
of the thousand lights twinkling on boats floating in Venetian
fêtes upstream and downstream.

On the Berkshire shore at Marlow, above the boathouses of
Messrs Meakes and Redknap, a massive royal coat of arms
was displayed. Once part of the Queen's barge and now
renovated, it presumably owed its presence there to Mr
Redknap who was one of the Queen's watermen. Meakes, in
1886, had a huge iron launch-house to accommodate his
steamers.

Beyond Marlow lock and Marlow islands, and the shining
curves of water overlooked by the Quarry Woods where in
late April first one then another tree broke into delicate leaf
against the sombre background of the mass until, as it were in
the twinkling of an eye, from those solitary torches the whole
was swept by the soft green flames of spring—beyond this
reach, downstream at Bourne End, stood the next little
scattering of boat-builders' yards. Shaw's had premises there.
Barges were built at Spade Oak, where the smell of pitch and
tar used in their making was noted with pleasure by Leslie.
Near Horsham's boatyard, the business of Messrs Townsend
flourished for many years on the riverside. Lacey's and
Llewellyn's works at Cookham were both taken over by Turk
in 1912.

Maidenhead was of course a great centre for the building
and letting of boats and launches, and as a boat-letting centre
became considerably more expensive than relatively less
fashionable places such as Hampton. H. Woodhouse (who
was to become the proprietor of the Thames Hotel) was
sufficiently well established by 1882 to be showing a punt and
canoe 'constructed on the most improved principles' at the
Sportsman's Exhibition at the Agricultural Hall in London,
where he sold several boats. By 1898 he had twelve launches,

one of which had been hired by no less a personage than the Queen of the Sandwich Islands. About 1890 his charge for letting steamers (including the *Queen of the Thames* which could take 150) was two guineas a day. When he started business there were only one or two such vessels on the Maidenhead part of the river and he was partly responsible for the huge increase in their numbers, having built many both small and large, some of the private ones being 'very handsome indeed'. Mr Grenfell was among his punt customers—in itself the highest recommendation, for the custom of that eagle-eyed punting champion was worth the praises of a score of lesser men. The two Misses Woodhouse were 'very graceful punt propellers and pretty scullers', having a wide choice of boats, for their father had works not only at Bray and Maidenhead but also at Staines.

In 1899 Woodhouse was expanding again, building a very large boathouse and dressing-rooms on his ground above Boulters, and naming his latest launch *A.M.B.* (Absent-minded Beggar) like Wilder's punt. The new boathouse, described as one of the best of its kind on the river, was ornamented by a long balcony giving a view of the Cliveden woods, and a central clock. No sooner was he established in these new premises than his Bray boathouse was destroyed by fire with the loss of one steamer and thirteen or fourteen boats, punts, canoes and oars.

In 1891 Mr Woodhouse was the victim of an act of petty crime not unusual on the river. Having hired out a fully-equipped canoe, he waited in vain for its return, and the following morning received a postcard giving no address but stating that the canoe had been left with the keeper of Bray lock. It had been stripped of its cushions, carpet and paddles and, needless to say, no payment was forthcoming; but it appears that boat firms were sufficiently sure of the honesty of the vast majority of their customers not to ask for deposits on such occasions. A Mr Rose, who makes a brief appearance in Thames history at this period showing an electric launch and punt at a yachting exhibition at the Royal Aquarium, Westminster, in 1899, was however even less lucky with one of his customers, a Mr Cohen of Hampstead, for whom he had built a punt. Mr Cohen had, it appears, made out that Rose was trying to overcharge him by £5, of which extortion he had expressed his disapproval by the satisfying but illegal method of giving the boat-builder a black eye, knocking him down, and hitting him on the back.

In 1900 an article appeared in the *Sketch* recounting memories of Maidenhead in the author's youth when Davis, a tailor who kept Boulters lock, opened it to probably less than a dozen boats in a week, when such a thing as a houseboat was never seen or even heard of, when silence brooded over the river path through Taplow Woods to Cliveden, and when Cookham was a village 'deliciously retired'. 'Jonathan Bond', recalled the author, 'let out the boats at the bridge-side and farmed a bit as well; there were scores of Bonds and gipsy-looking Andrews in punts and wherries and outriggers; the fishermen *par excellence* were old Simon Wilder and his son Harry.'

Bonds, Andrews and Wilders all flourished in the Golden Age of the Thames, and Andrews was more than once summoned to place his launches at the service of royalty. His business, which was the first to hire out boats at Maidenhead, was originally established in 1821, but had been allowed to go into decline until revived and built up by Ned Andrews, the grandson of the founder. Ned's first love was fishing, for which he made all his own tackle, and he was an ex-professional punting champion, 'splendidly "put together", and always in hard condition, his steely sinews being indeed a sight when in play', his countenance 'genial, though resolute'. In his young days, after his father's untimely death, he had known what it was to want a meal, but by 1890 those days were far behind him, for by then, with his 'natty' boathouse next to the Brigade of Guards Boat Club, he owned 'about a hundred handsome and completely equipped boats, punts and canoes, of all descriptions'. By 1891 he was building a new boathouse, and in 1897 exhibited five boats at the Yachting Exhibition at the Royal Aquarium, Westminster; he had just built showrooms and residence with balconies overlooking the river near Taplow mills. The Misses Andrews made punt and boat cushions for the business and did the upholstering. Their father's steamers included *Ned*, *Nell*, *Bertha* and *Nip-Nip*; his electric launches *Bleak* and *Gudgeon*; and he could accommodate hundreds of boats. *Ned* was hired for use on a Scottish loch one summer. The steamer, its captain and his assistant set off by train from Taplow, leaving their familiar stream amid the gentle southern chalklands to float in the shadow of lofty and majestic mountains of the north. Andrews hired out 150 small craft and no less than seventeen launches on Ascot Sunday 1905. All his launches were out too on Ascot Sunday 1909, at an average of ten guineas each for the day. Far from Mr Andrews then was the spectre of poverty!

In 1910, however, Andrews like Woodhouse before him suffered a severe fire. Damage was estimated at over £3,000. Seven electric launches were destroyed including two which had been on exhibition at Olympia, a new gig, several boats and punts and 350 larch poles from which punt poles were to have been made. Many motors and a new lathe, fittings and tools were rendered useless.

Harry Wilder in 1885 was engaged in levelling land he had acquired on the river bank, placing a wall along its edge, and building a boathouse and shops. In 1891 the *Lock to Lock Times* informed its readers: 'Mr Wilder's new boathouse at Maidenhead will be completed in about a week's time, and then will be found replete with dressing-room and every other convenience for boating.' The firm had started in 1881 in a small way, but by his death in 1910 had become one of the largest of its kind on the Upper Thames, with over 200 boats. Harry Wilder, like his father before him, had been a famous professional fisherman (said once to have landed a salmon near Bray). He had been judge at many regattas and punting races, head bailiff of the Maidenhead, Cookham and Bray Angling Association, 'almost, if not quite, *facile princeps*' among the Thames professional fishermen—described variously as 'the king-fisher' and the 'Trout-catching Machine'— 'erect and wiry of frame with a clear, keen eye'. The Gospel story of the miraculous draught of fishes was read at his funeral when he was laid to rest at an advanced age in Maidenhead cemetery; by this time his son Henry John was

established at their 'elegant and truly artistic boat-house'
between Maidenhead bridge and the New Thames Hotel,
there presiding over as perfect a collection of craft as ever
gladdened the eye of a rowing man.

Bond, like Wilder, was busy building about 1885, when he
erected a spacious balconied launch-house opposite Skindles.
About five years later Maidenhead Corporation decided it
was getting too little income from its land by the bridge which
he rented for less than £10 per annum, and put it up for
public auction. After this he had to pay no less than £280 per
annum for a smaller area. There could be no clearer proof of
the prosperity which the Golden Age of the Thames brought
to riverside towns. 'This patriarch of Thames boatbuilders',
as the *Maidenhead Advertiser* described Jonathan Bond, who
died in 1892, was one of the first to make boat-letting a
distinct business at Maidenhead, and lived to own a fleet.
Shortly before his death he had constructed a steam launch
which, readers were told, produced the 'merest wrinkle' on
the water when going at full speed. Some years later the firm
built the *Empress of India*, a vessel bearing the name (as the
mayor of Maidenhead said at her champagne launching) of
'the greatest woman who ever lived'. She could sleep 8, dine
50 at a sitting, accommodate 250, and was capable of going to
sea. *His Majesty*, new for the 1906 season, was even larger. A
few years later the number of boats to be let at Maidenhead
during the Henley regatta period was such that supply
exceeded demand, but business was flourishing again the
following Ascot Sunday when Bonds were hiring extra punts
and launches from other up-river firms. Latecomers on Ascot
Sunday 1913 found little chance of hiring a boat anywhere
between Richmond and Marlow.

The building and letting of launches was a Windsor
industry also, catering for Eton's wetbobs. At Eton itself
Winter's boathouses erected about 1890 were a great improvement on the old tumbledown wooden sheds. Whites of
Windsor found 1891 a prosperous season for houseboats, and
a boat-builder was setting up at Datchet for the first time. By
1885 boat-building was constantly increasing at Staines.
Immisch's electric-launch works were situated on two large

aits between Molesey and Sunbury, and at Sunbury steamers fuelled with Welsh coal awaited hire. Turks were at Kingston; Messums at Richmond.

The Thames Boat Builders Protection Association dated from 1885, and in 1900 was reported to be flourishing. A couple of years later they initiated an exhibition, which they hoped would be an annual event, at Earls Court. Many of the best-known firms were represented, including Andrews who had two electric launches on display. The latest models of launch motors were also shown. About this time launch employees and watermen united to form a branch of the Up-River Legal Protection Society. A weekly subscription of 4d covered them for legal assistance and protection and enabled the society to make an allowance towards its members' funeral expenses. The importance of watermen was greater than the humble nature of their calling might seem to imply, for on their smartness or carelessness, sullenness or civility, depended visitors' first impressions of the adventure of boating on the Thames. At a watermen's dinner at the Compleat Angler in 1886 they were complimented upon their efficiency and general good behaviour which did so much to make the vicinity of Marlow popular. As boat businesses expanded, so the trade of waterman gave more and more employment, and a letter to the *Maidenhead Advertiser* early in the new century suggested a uniform for boatmen who, the writer complained, looked shabby and detracted from the brilliance of the scene.

Maidenhead's watermen recited popular poems of the day at their annual dinner at the Thames Hotel in 1888, descending from the painful melodrama of 'Christmas Day in the Workhouse' to long, comforting pulls from their glasses as toasts were drunk with musical honours.

22

ROWING, PUNTING AND SAILING

One day early in 1910 a bitter wind stirred the beeches of the Quarry Woods. Their branches, bearing tiny buds close sheathed to needle-sharp tips, swayed against the sky. The buds awaited the welling of the sap, and the expanse of Cockmarsh, with its greater and its lesser tumulus where the grasses bent before the wind's onslaught, awaited the green vividness of May. On the river eight young men strained over their blades as with pounding hearts and swelling muscles they forced their racing boat through the now inhospitable waters. On the river bank Mr E. Butler, the proprietor of the Quarry Hotel where the eight, the Cambridge boat-race crew, the 'Cantabs', were putting up during their few days' practice rowing on the Thames, turned up his coat collar and shivered as he watched his illustrious guests; the wind cut him like a knife.

Mr Butler caught a chill that day which led to his death at the age of forty-four by the feverish path of double pneumonia. Yet when the 'Cantabs' and their rivals 'the dark blues' appeared on the Upper Thames to practise during late winter days for their famous race (staying at the Quarry Hotel, the Ferry Inn at Cookham, at Eton or with well-known habitués of the river—Mr Grenfell at Taplow Court, Colonel Ricardo or Mr H. Gold of Cookham, Mr R. C. Lehmann, who had had a book published on rowing, or Mr C. Hammersley of Bourne End) crowds braved the cold to turn out and watch them. At Marlow one year spectators included equestrians, ladies, and a man on crutches. The Oxford crew were 'lustily cheered' by workers at Bourne End's paper mills, and Mr Lehmann had a handsome boathouse erected at his house, Fieldhead, to accommodate the Cantabs' boat. Mr Grenfell on foot and Mr Lehmann on a bicycle coached crews from the bank; Dr Warre of Eton combined the functions of coach and cox.

PLATE 26 'The Chaperone' (*Delightful Thames* by E. D. Manning)

PLATE 27 Henley regatta crowds assembling at Paddington station in
about 1910

PLATE 28 A royal tea party al fresco on Monkey Island

In 1881, for a cost of £2,600, what was described as perhaps the finest accommodation for boats on the Thames was built for the Oxford University Boat Club opposite the new mouth of the Cherwell, cut some years before to allow water to escape at flood time. No sooner was it erected than it was burnt down in suspicious circumstances with its valuable contents, rowlocks alone surviving among the debris. The water bailiff's dog, tied up in a corner, lost its innocent life.

Rowing clubs were formed up and down the Middle Thames, although the *Lock to Lock Times* noted with surprise that there was none in Abingdon in 1891, and shortly after this Wallingford's had to be dissolved owing to a lack of members and funds. Reading's club dates from 1867. Henley's was already well established by mid-Victorian days; and Leander, the oldest on the Thames, its membership drawn from the public schools and universities, built a residential club and boathouse at Henley in the 1890s. Marlow's rowing club was founded in 1871 and flourished throughout the Golden Age. Among its founders was W. J. Shone, a local surgeon and veteran of the Crimea War and Indian Mutiny, carrying to the quiet banks of the Thames (as innumerable others carried to every British town and city, village and remotest hamlet) memories of the glories and tragedies of Empire. To the accompaniment of the town band, 'The Boys of the Old Brigade' was sung at the club's annual dinner in the Compleat Angler's marquee in 1884; in 1900 several members had enlisted, and one had been killed in the South African War; and in 1914 all the members of the eight which had rowed at Henley were serving their country. In due course a total of forty-eight club members enlisted.

Cookham Rowing Club was reported to be growing in 1884. Maidenhead's club, founded in the 1870s, had mixed fortunes. It was handicapped by the distance of the river from the town's centre, but enough members had joined, and paid their subscriptions, by 1884, to put the idea into the head of a committee member that it would be profitable to abscond with the funds, which he did forthwith. That same year another committee member, a clergyman, had occasion to drop a friendly hint at the club's annual dinner suggesting that there should be no impropriety of language or conduct to bring discredit on them or alienate would-be members or supporters, while a vice-president said 'there should be nothing whatever in the shape of ungentlemanly behaviour on the part of any member of the club'. Apart from the report that there had been some 'improprieties', no information is to be found, and whether these misdemeanours represented a few 'damn's too audibly uttered' or bore closer resemblance to the conduct of 'Arry in his cups, must remain for ever a mystery.

Maidenhead Rowing Club had the great advantage of the active interest of Mr Grenfell. By 1892 membership was declining on account of unsatisfactory accommodation, and the club set itself to raise funds to build a new boathouse near the bridge. A smoking concert was held at a hall comfortably furnished with easy chairs and occasional tables bearing pot plants, and as the blue smoke rose, the jolly strains of 'Mrs 'Enery 'Awkins' competed with the tattoo of rain on the roof. Invitation balls too were held to raise money, and by 1897 the building was paid for and three new boats acquired: members now possessed 'as pretty a little clubhouse as could be found on the Thames'. At the annual dinner, after grace, toasts were drunk to the Queen and the royal family and a verse of the National Anthem sung to piano accompaniment. 'Kathleen Mavourneen', 'Only to See Her Face Again' and 'Remember Me' followed. The club was in the doldrums in 1900; owing to members leaving the town, some for South African battlefields, they had no crew at their own regatta. In 1901 the club was almost defunct, but by the next year it had revived.

Eton College, the 'best nursery of rowing in England', had a well-equipped boat club which by 1893 possessed a sizeable stock of boats including a ten-oar. The town's Excelsior Rowing Club was opening its season in 1892 by proceeding, chiefly by water, to Monkey Island, 'where they partook of their annual spread at Host Plummer's'. Kingston Rowing Club was described as the only localised club of importance between Oxford and Putney. There were other rowing clubs in the town. The Royal Canoe Club, based in London and boasting Prince Tum-tum for commodore, held a week's regatta at Bourne End in 1894, and that same portly prince expressed an interest in the efforts being made to revive Thames sculling. By 1901 a Skiff Racing Association was being set up, and a few years later the Upper Thames Skiff Club, based at Shiplake, was reported to be in flourishing condition. A member of the East Molesey Skiff Club appeared at Maidenhead in 1911, having punted there in just over seven hours, with a short rest at Windsor.

If one of the hazards of training for rowing races was the possibility of a humiliating, not to say painful, outcrop of boils, often on 'the seat of honour', champion punters too faced arduous periods of practice and self-discipline before they could hope to aspire to amateur or professional titles. For a number of years, Mr Grenfell, and Abel Beesley who had trained him, held respectively the amateur and professional championship titles, until they resigned to give others a chance. Mr Grenfell, chairman of the Thames Punting Club's committee after the club's reorganisation in 1890, was largely responsible for the popularity of punting, and Beesley too had done much to bring it into prominence. The professional championship was instituted in 1886 at Maidenhead, where gravel gave the river bed a suitable surface—despite the fact that, as Mr Grenfell remarked in a speech, although Britannia ruled the waves she did not appear to be able to rule the bottom of the Thames as there were holes and other conditions which made it difficult to get a fair course. These difficulties did not trouble Beesley, however, as he stood on the Cliveden bank one summer's day in 1892 smoking his pipe as he waited for an opponent who was late; then, watched by a crowd of several hundred, set off in a new racing punt—18in across the widest part, borrowed from Mr Grenfell—and using a pole weighing only 6¾lb, stopping from time to time to allow his opponent to catch up with him, amusing himself by using alternately the top and bottom of his pole, chatting with spectators, and putting on a final spurt to show his paces and win by twenty lengths.

The following year, twenty-five competitors assembled at Maidenhead to take part in the professional punting championship races. Mr Grenfell acted as starter, the beginning of

each race being marked by the sound of artillery fired by Mr
Sam Shorter, a familiar figure on such aquatic occasions. The
Thames Conservancy launch kept the course clear, and large
crowds saw Charlie Asplen of Maidenhead shoot first past the
winning post to the strains of 'See the Conquering Hero
Comes'. The next professional championship race saw a good
deal of money change hands. Both competitors appeared
done up at the finish of the race, and a cloud hung over the
occasion for it was suggested that the result may have been
prearranged. For five consecutive years before 1914
seventeen-stone F. Nicholes of Egham held the professional
title.

One year there was a boys' punting race, the prizes for
which were £1 and 15s orders from a local outfitter for
clothing. A gold medal and money prizes were presented to
adult professional champions, and although Maidenhead was
the punting centre of the Thames, contests also took place at
Hampton Court and Shepperton.

The ladies were ardent supporters of competitors for the
amateur punting title. At Maidenhead in 1894:

> . . . they ran along the Buckinghamshire bank and made the
> woods resound with musical shouts to their favourites, and they
> proved themselves quite as good runners and supporters as the
> sterner sex. It was certainly not the fault of the ladies if their
> gentleman friends did not win.

Meanwhile, a band 'discoursed' sweet music from the *Queen
of the Thames*, and afterwards members of the Thames
Punting Club and members of the fourth estate climbed the
wooded hillside whose trees wore the sober greens of August,
and passed under the dark boughs of Taplow Court's Cedar
Walk to partake of a 'recherché' repast at the mansion.

Beesley's 77-year-old uncle won £50 for a punting contest
against a 66-year-old, and Beesley's cousin was a pioneer lady
punter. The *West End Review* carried an article on punting
for ladies in 1897. The new method of 'pricking' rather than
walking the length of the boat was considered a graceful form
of exercise calculated to improve the physique. Many young
girls were reported to have grown perceptibly stronger,

straighter, and even taller, after six weeks or two months of punting, which developed the right muscles and exercised every part of the body, whereas sculling, remarked the writer severely but with justice, was unbecoming, causing scullers to get heated and shine with a heightened colour. James Englefield, in his *Delightful Life of Pleasure on the Thames*, described the challenges and mysteries of the art of punting, requiring:

> . . . near and far-sightedness, nerve, strength, exact judgement to balance, steady, and keep the smoothly-gliding craft straight, and skill (only to be gained by much practice) where to place the punt pole in order to commence its propelling stroke, and at the finish of that, to lift the iron-shod end as noiselessly as possible, so as to prevent it grating along the gravelly bottom, and disturbing the fish, and by it at the same time guide the punt aright, turn it to, or stop it, at the required destination.

Sailing was popular, too. At Oxford in the 1880s it was the subject of not altogether approving comment in A. J. Church's *Isis and Thamesis*, although he noticed with a certain relief that 'the sailing-boats, whose wild career used to be a terror in former days to the throngs of rowers on the lower river', had been 'banished or removed by common consent' to the reaches above the city. 'It is a well-known fact', he added, 'that an Englishman has a great need, especially when he is young, of being protected against himself. He dearly loves to spice his pleasures with the sense of danger . . . and the river fascinates him most when he can discern a prospect of being drowned.'

The *Lock to Lock Times* carried an article in 1891 on boat-sailing above lock. The writer commented that little of the boat race was visible to the watching John Bull, whereas:

> . . . he may see, on any fine Saturday afternoon that he likes to choose in the early summer or through the autumn, a spectacle much more artistically beautiful, one which may be watched from start to finish without shifting more than a hundred yards, and which takes place in pure air, amid lovely surroundings . . . he will find, shortly before the reasonable hour of 3pm, a little fleet of white-winged boats, impatiently awaiting the signal of that

patient and most indispensable gentleman, 'the officer of the day' . . . And what a pretty sight it is!

Sailing boats had by that time become so expensive that clubs suffered a consequent shortage of sailing members, for:

> . . . men, in the opening years of their lives, have not always a hundred or a hundred and twenty pounds to spare, and when that delightful period does come, the inclination for boats and boating has passed away. And a man who, once thoroughly impregnated with the taste for sailing, would have gone on, to his own benefit and the increase of a wholesome and healthy sport, is left to the vices of carpet slippers, armchairs, and cards, and dies of apoplexy ten years sooner than he would have done had he kept his pipes open by exercise in the fresh air.

At Bourne End, where the gentle inland cliff of Winter Hill overlooks the grassy sea of Cockmarsh, the Upper Thames Sailing Club was founded in 1884. A sailing club was formed at Reading not long after, and in due course plans were afoot for a club at Cookham. But Bourne End, where a new headquarters was opened in 1890, remained the most important centre for sailing on the upper river, flourishing despite the increased cost of boats. Yachtsmen from other clubs converged there for the annual Bourne End week, when they competed for the Queen's Challenge cup modelled on an old flagon dug up near Smyrna, and were entertained to luncheons of a recherché character presided over by the commodore, Colonel Fitzroy Clayton. Colonel Clayton had to swim for his life during a race in 1904 when thunder cracked overhead, lightning unseamed the sky, torrential rain pitted the surface of the usually placid waters, and his boat, blown over on to its side, came to rest on the river bed. But then A. J. Church did not exclude the more mature Englishman from his strictures. 'He dearly loves to spice his pleasures with the sense of danger . . . and the river fascinates him most when he can discern a prospect of being drowned.'

23

RESPECTABLE SWIMMING AND
INDECENT BATHING

T. C. Easton, the honorary secretary of the Professional Swimming Association, entered the river at Oxford one September morning in 1890, and struck out downstream. He intended to swim at least as far as Teddington, covering an average of sixteen miles per day. The following morning, after he had been on his way for about three hours, his leg was held in the agonising vice of cramp, and this torture he fought for a further two hours, surrendering finally at Moulsford bridge where he dragged himself on to the bank, his face white with pain. Again he set out the next day but, developing a swelling on his leg, was forced to abandon the attempt.

Madame Mitchell of Kingston Baths astonished the gaping populace of that town in the summer of 1888 by not only going through a hoop on the river bed but also eating and drinking under water. Swimming was taken seriously though at Eton, and college boys using the river were required to pass a test, taking a header into the water, and using breast stroke to show their ability to keep afloat both with and against the current, swimming also on their backs, and treading water with their hands held high. The lower boys bathed at Cuckoo Weir in a backwater, and Mitton described the trials taking place there: 'a set of trembling pink youngsters stand in a punt ready to take a graceful header, or from sheer nervousness, to fall with an ugly flop smack upon the water and be disqualified for the time being!' Seniors swam at 'Athens', a part of the river railed off and provided with ladders. The Eton and Windsor Royal Humane Society held annual swimming matches at 'Athens', and in 1891 paraded the streets of Windsor in advance of these competitions, stepping it out to the strains of the town's brass band 'which played some inspiriting marches'. Despite this attractive advertisement 'the more respectable part of the community', it seems, failed to support the event. A similar reluctance to plunge into the watery element was displayed by 74-year-old Bob Allen, a local boat-builder, who had undertaken to race 200yd against 76-year-old Jimmy Slade, the 'Windsor Guide'. The heart of the recalcitrant Bob failed him at the last moment, and having divested himself of his boots he remained obstinately clothed while his senior, who was made of sterner stuff, struck out alone amid the cheers of the onlookers.

Long-distance races, upstream to Cookham or down to Bray, took place under the auspices of Maidenhead Amateur Swimming Club, and boys were encouraged to take part in competitions. Over a thousand spectators watched boys competing for a shield in 1907. Another year the club planned an aquatic entertainment, to include blindfold and Siamese races, and a tournament. There was a swimming club at Cookham; the Otter Club made regular visits to race at Bourne End (partaking of a capital meat tea afterwards at the Railway Tavern in 1888); at Henley there was a bathing place at Solomon's Hatch below Marsh lock. Reading too had its bathing place, a walled-in section of the river near Caversham lock. At Oxford in 1891 a swimming and water polo club was being set up under the presidency of that great rowing man Lord Ampthill; and a little further upstream Thacker noted some years later a part set aside for swimming. Pangbourne weir pool served excellently for this purpose, 'and the lockkeeper will supply towels and drawers for a small consideration'. Shiplake's lock-keeper performed a similar service. Just upstream from Teddington lock another bathing place was established and those at Windsor, Reading and Abingdon were reserved for the use of ladies at certain hours.

Mr Bickerdyke, so fertile of complaints, complained of the little corrugated iron enclosures for swimming which disfigured the river at Henley and Wallingford. Dickens, on the other hand, enumerating the dangers to be faced even at such established swimming places as Odney Pool at Cookham, commented on the failure of local authorities to provide places where the public might bathe in safety. The question was a vexed one, for much of the river bank was privately owned or near enough to private property to make public bathing there unwelcome to riparian owners and the few remaining sites were mainly ill-situated. Swimmers had to compete with all the other interests using the river and its banks for business or pleasure—boats and barges, anglers and excursionists. Not only could they get in the way, but some of them, as we shall see, caused the bosoms of passers-by so to swell with indignation that they well nigh burst with the pressure of it.

At Cookham in 1876, for the third time in thirty years, the villagers were defending their right to bathe at Odney, this time against a Miss Fleming, who was trying to establish a private right to the site. Shortly afterwards the secretary of the local swimming club was writing to the *Maidenhead Advertiser* that the 'lawyers, policemen, and the members of the lower order imported into the village' over the August bank holiday weekend had failed to deter bathers, and a circular was issued asking all 'good men and true' to subscribe to a defence fund. As on earlier occasions, an action for trespass had been started against one of the protesting villagers.

The Odney bathing place appears to have weathered this storm, and in 1901 the public-spirited Mr E. Cooper, who was later responsible for the erection of a flood barrier between Maidenhead and Cookham, was trying in vain to get support for a ladies' bathing place. Dredging and the building of a dam further downstream would have been necessary, and in due course the presence of an attendant, and perhaps an addition to the rates was feared. One local resident suggested that the well-to-do might not wish to bathe with common people; another, who had settled at Cookham because of the absence of the usual riverside crowd, feared an influx of visitors. But the scheme emerged again a few years later when Cookham ladies were forming a club to swim near Odney Pool. The arrangements were short-lived, however, for under the heading 'The Nymphs Must Wait', the *Maidenhead Advertiser* reported that Sir George Young by cutting away a dam had spoilt the pool, saying it infringed his rights as a commoner and owner of adjacent property, and emphasising his point by pulling down and throwing into the river a dressing-tent on a nearby island.

At Maidenhead in 1861 there was a public bathing place with a 1d admission charge, in the river near the gasworks (an eyesore described by one writer as 'that crown of thorns on nature's head'), but the site was in due course taken for building. Later Mr Woodhouse, the hotelier, enclosed a piece of water and charged 1s for admission, or 1s 6d for a weekly ticket. At first he kept it open until 9.30pm, then closed at 8.30 because of the lack of patronage which resulted from charges far beyond the reach of the humble wage-earner. At Maidenhead the bathing place problem was discussed many times over the years, but no lasting or satisfactory arrangement resulted, although a swimming pool was opened in the town. At Marlow in 1883 a meeting was held to consider setting up a bathing place there, and it was pointed out that many people had no facilities for washing themselves properly except in the Thames. A site was found, but the owners of the necessary ground refused to part with it, and by the following summer it seems that nothing had been done except that Mr Foottit had arranged for a bathing place for his visitors at the Compleat Angler. Later there were two places for swimming at Marlow.

Cottagers, to whose picturesque but cramped dwellings water had to be carried from town or village pumps, naturally took advantage of the bountiful supply which nature sent flowing near their doors. Whether for washing or swimming, regardless of the existence or otherwise of bathing places, they plunged into the river. Many did not 'condescend to wear drawers', thus giving rise to the phenomenon known as indecent bathing, and it is difficult to imagine that they did not enjoy the thunderous indignation which this practice brought bursting forth from their betters, indignation which came pouring out in a bubbling torrent of print, 'with the result', as the *Lock to Lock Times* pointed out:

> ... that the disgusting state of things goes on exactly the same as ever ... The lads and men who render certain parts of the Thames a purgatory for the river's fairer frequenters are not of a

class which cares one iota for the criticisms of the newspapers, however severe they may be.

A correspondent wrote to the *Maidenhead Advertiser* in 1881: 'I could have imagined myself in one of the Pacific Islands, on the banks of the Nile, or, indeed, anywhere save amongst a community calling itself "civilised".' The paper commented:

> If the police fail to restore propriety to the river bank and comfort to its frequenters, our only alternative will be to send down a few cases of Nubian blacking; with attendants ready to apply it to the white barbarians, and so make their appearance consistent with their habits.

Three years later, the *Advertiser* was informing its readers:

> There is a spot on the river-bank . . . which has fallen into a state of barbarism. It is a locality to which boating-parties give a wide berth, and which they pass with averted eyes. Someone, however—'one low churl, compact of thankless earth'—has gazed and counted, and he informs us that no fewer than 104 men, boys, and lads disported themselves there in shameless disregard of civilised proprieties, on Thursday evening. There would probably be some abuse of this kind even if a proper bathing place were constructed, but with this provision made, no excuse would remain for tolerating such an affront on decency as is now committed, and the police could act with determination to suppress the abuse. As it is, something should be done to keep the offence within the narrowest limits.

The occupants of a rowing boat, seeing a launch which had broken down, seized what they must have considered a golden opportunity to annoy the occupants of that stranded monster. As the indignant owner wrote to the *Lock to Lock Times*:

> . . . seeing we had a lady on board—my wife—they pulled their boat ashore within about twenty yards of us and then commenced to strip themselves, which done, they sported with one another in the way that I think only English blackguards would under the circumstances.

Offending the fair sex was fine sport. One indecent bather tried to unship the rudder of a boat containing ladies; at Eton another 'savage' left the water when a boat with ladies came past.

A letter headed 'Cussedness on the Upper Thames' complained:

> As matters are at present, the ubiquitous bather is an intolerable nuisance. In avoiding the rock of Scylla with one or two bathers around it, you are as likely as not to run into the whirlpool of Charybdis with fifty demons in their birthday suits floundering about and yelling red language with fiendish delight.

'Disgusted' wrote to complain about the situation between Reading and Caversham: 'It is simply a disgrace to the Authorities that they allow the public to be so gratuitously insulted and to have their sense of decency so flagrantly abused.' The problem was of course worse near towns than in country districts, and Dickens explained how in one case 'a vigilante committee of the able-bodied residents took the matter into their own hands, and by the summary chastisement of some of the sturdiest and most audacious offenders very speedily worked a signal and permanent cure'.

Marlow, before places were set aside for bathing there, suffered severely. In 1878 an offender who had disported himself on the bridge pleaded in defence, when brought up before a local magistrate, that no ladies had been present. On another occasion a bather clambered out of the water after his dip and lay naked on the river bank reading the *Daily Mail*, for which indulgence he was fined £1. Not only boys but men 'disgraced civilisation' by running about in the nude, apparently to dry themselves.

Indecent bathers, like 'Arries, were a twofold cause of trouble. Visually annoying and financially profitless, they set local residents on edge for fear that their presence might discourage the high class visitors who were the chief source of income to those who lived by the river trade. In the summer of 1881, Marlow tradesmen petitioned their magistrates on the subject in a 'numerously signed' memorandum which stated:

> In addition to the annoyance which is caused to all respectable people by the appearance of large numbers of naked persons,

language of the most indecent and disgusting description is daily indulged in by the bathers, and reference made to ladies who happen to be passing either up or down the river in boats.

Fines for indecent bathing became payable under Thames Conservancy bylaws later in the 1880s, and efforts were made to restrict swimming to early morning or late evening hours. Roughs at Long Ditton who had no sense of decency were discovered bathing before the permitted hour (9pm), a youth was convicted at Datchet, two were seen bathing 'in a state of nudity' at Cleeve, while at Remenham a naughty boy tore the canvas screen which had been set up only the previous week, in response to several letters from the Thames Conservancy, to conceal bathers too clearly visible from the frequently passing boats. Indecent bathers were prosecuted for horrifying the public at Cookham and at Monkey Island. Three Londoners were fined for 'bathing in a nude condition in full view of Bray lock', but some YMCA boys down on an excursion from Ealing escaped with the payment of costs as they did not know they were doing wrong.

In 1887, after the site of the Maidenhead bathing place had been taken for building, the local debating society chose as its subject the bathing place question. One of the speakers pointed out that 'certain Eton aristocrats' were free to bathe at Windsor at all hours, regardless of passing boats. Were the aquatic gambols of the aristocracy, by some mysterious alchemy (a variation perhaps of that 'divinity doth hedge a king'), rendered less obtrusive than the cavortings of the common man?

24

DROWNINGS

We turn now from all glinting, sunlit aspects of the river, from all moods and feelings, severe, laughing or pensive, which the river and its users engendered in those who judged as one secure of life judges his fellows, to look through different eyes, eyes before whose vision the waters are swept with the dark wings of death. So many terrible, desperate, hopeless struggles for life took place there in solitude or before the gaze of helpless lookers-on, that, to one who knows its history, the Thames' gentle surface appears as to De Quincey in opium-heightened dreams the sea: 'paved with innumerable faces, upturned to the heavens: faces imploring, wrathful, despairing, surged upwards by thousands, by myriads, by generations, by centuries'.

Death by drowning during the Golden Age of the Thames was due to many causes. A large proportion of those who ventured on the river could not swim, but even experienced swimmers and people well used to handling boats were sometimes caught by currents or eddies. If ladies were submerged, their long dresses impeded them, and one who fell in during the era of hobble skirts narrowly escaped paying with her life for following that foolish fashion. Some victims of drowning capsized when boating, some missed their way in darkness or fog, some overbalanced, some were skylarking, some were tipsy and missed their footing. Others were swept away by floods, or lowered their punt poles into ballast holes. Some stepped into ballast holes when bathing, or swam too soon after a meal, or were seized with cramp. And some threw up their hands and sank from sight for no apparent reason. The river is haunted with their dying words, and their graves are to be found in the green churchyards of riverside towns and villages.

For the ferryman, the lock-keeper and their families, death by drowning was little short of an occupational hazard. The body of the Gatehampton ferryman was recovered from the river in 1879, and G. Collins the Cookham ferryman drowned on duty in 1881. Collins overbalanced in darkness and pouring rain, using two poles, one shorter than the other. A splash and noise of struggling were heard, and his voice gasping 'Jesus! Jesus!', but he was invisible in the blackness of the night. After a short time nothing more was heard but the rain dashing itself against the river's surface. His successor too, a 'sober, respectable man' in his sixties, died tragically in January 1893, but into the tragedy of his death entered a touch of farce. He arrived home after an excursion to buy pigsmeat for supper, went to an outhouse to get a frying pan, and did not return. Despite the fact that 'there was proper closet accommodation at the ferry cottage', this man was wont to go to his boat of a night for (in the *Maidenhead Advertiser*'s delicate phrase) 'a certain purpose'. The flap of his trousers was found to be unbuttoned when his body was eventually recovered over a month later from the mill stream near Odney Pool, where the current had taken it. It is interesting to note the appetite for horrors of an age commonly discreet and restrained in its public expressions, for the description generally used in such cases was 'the body presented a sickening spectacle'. In 1893 also at Keen Edge Ferry, upstream from Shillingford, both the ferryman and his wife lost their lives.

The Hurley lock-keeper drowned in 1869, and some years earlier his wife had had a narrow escape owing to the dilapidated state of the lock-side. The Whitchurch keeper and his son were both lost in 1871, the Pinkhill keeper missing, presumed drowned, in 1881, the Abingdon and the Caversham keepers lost in 1883, the Shiplake keeper in 1890. One very dark evening in December 1890, the Hambledon keeper was going round the lock as usual to see that all was safe. Crossing a narrow unprotected ledge by the gates, he fell, and his wife hearing the splash threw a buoy in the direction of the sound. Apparently he failed to grasp it. A collection was made for his family, which by the following March had reached £183 2s 6d. The wife of the Bell Weir keeper died in her lock in 1899.

The new century brought further tragedies. In 1909 the
only child of A. Wise of Hurley lock was found drowned. He
could handle a boat well for such a little boy, for he had seen
only four summers. During the winter of 1910–11 A. Almond,
previously at Boulters and then newly appointed to Radcot,
was found dead in the river after floods. His successor, Alfred
Beesley (formerly at St John's and Buscot), lost his wife in the
waters there one dark and bitter night the following winter;
two of his boys had been drowned while he was at Lechlade.
The Teddington lock-keeper also lost a son by drowning.

Temple lock was a place fraught with tragedy. In the
summer of 1888 the 11-year-old daughter of W. J. Wood, the
keeper there, fell in from the small bridge on the lock gates.
The coroner's inquest reported praiseworthy efforts 'to
rescue the little one from the roaring waters, particularly by a
gentleman from Brixton . . . but all efforts to save life were
unavailing'. Grace Simpkins, aged 14, 'a very bright and
promising girl', daughter of a later keeper, drowned by her
father's lock as the result of a curious accident in 1908. A
gardener at Temple Lodge on the opposite side of the river
noticed her girlish figure, perhaps with admiration, as she
cycled along the towpath going home from school one day in
early summer. She was carrying a milk can. Suddenly he saw
her pitch headlong into the river, flung down his tools and
rushed to tell her father. They searched together, and
Simpkins found his daughter's bicycle on the river bed near
the bank. 'A painful scene then ensued.' The body, which was
but a yard or two from the bank, was recovered with a
boathook and, when the inquest took place in Temple lock
garden which the previous summer had won first prize in the
gardens competition, it was suggested that the accident might
have been caused by the milk can being caught up in the
bicycle.

Many victims of drowning accidents worked on or by the
river, or lived on its banks, and of these the 20-year-old son of
Mr Thomas of Temple Mills must serve as a type. On a dark
autumn evening when doing something over one of the
'thoroughs', he slipped into the rushing waters. Rescue was
impossible, and although the mill was immediately stopped

his body was not recovered until the next morning. 'Brief life is here our portion' sang the choir of Bisham church at his funeral service and, as the procession slowly paced to the graveside, the lady organist played the solemn chords of the 'Dead March' in *Saul*.

From time to time during these years, under the heading 'Shocking Discovery', the finding was reported of a weighted parcel containing the body of a newborn child. Such tragedies speak for themselves.

Two little boys, who had lived among scenes so different that they might have been inhabitants of separate planets, died choking in Thames waters during the early years of this century. The horizons of one had been bounded by grey rows of mean houses until he came with a party from Bethnal Green School Board to spend a holiday by the Thames. Neither he nor his companions could swim, but despite this fact several of them went in the river, and he was drowned near Monkey Island. Major Burnham, DSO, a celebrated scout of the South African War, was staying with his 7-year-old son in a bungalow by Bourne End railway bridge. The small boy had been all over the world with his father and looked on scenes beyond the slum child's imagining. He could ride and shoot and had even been taken elephant shooting. He disappeared from the Bourne End garden where he had been playing with a little tin attached to a string. His father found this pathetic relic floating, and later his son's body was recovered.

Occasionally excursionists, whose knowledge of the river and its ways was slight, were drowned when swimming or boating, cut off in high-spirited mirth. A London cabinet-maker sank while bathing at Windsor and although Eton College boys dived to the rescue they were too late to restore him to life. Another excursionist drowned when he fell backwards from a steamer into Datchet Reach, and two waiters fell from another steamer, one being rescued although he sank like a log near Boulters, but the other drowning. A Frenchman, one of a party on the *Firefly*, fell in when attempting to dip water opposite Shiplake church, and could not be saved, as the season was winter, the stream rapid and high. A young sapper, the only son of a widowed mother whom he supported, overbalanced backwards during a trip on the steamer *His Majesty* as he sat on the railing talking to a friend. The sergeant major in charge would not allow any of the party to jump in to search for him because it was dark, but one of the crew was landed, ran along the bank, and returned in a punt. The body was not found until the next morning, its position (on its back) showing that the young soldier had made no struggle for life. Three volleys were sounded over his grave in Windsor cemetery as the 'Last Post' played him to rest—a sound to be heard in tragic circumstances times without number during the coming months and years, for the date was 1914.

Captain Norris, late of the South Wales Borderers, staying at the Compleat Angler, paid with his life for the foolish mistake of standing up in mid-stream in a small skiff to change oars with his companion. The boat overturned and his companion clung to it while the captain struck out for the bank, looking back to cry 'Hang tight, old chappie!' He disappeared before reaching land, and the Marlow Rowing Club four, just back from practice, were unable to find him in the failing light.

A triple tragedy occurred at Frogmill Island, Medmenham, where the headmaster of a London County Council school was camping with his two sons and some friends. One of his boys, after an early morning swim, cried 'Oh! I do feel awfully fagged!', but immediately plunged in again against the advice of his father, who, with the brother, died in a vain attempt to rescue him from drowning, having apparently become entangled in weeds. Their bodies were found in 7ft of water, a yard from a point where the water shallowed to 18in.

Steam launches, those villains of the river, became involved in drowning cases from time to time. At Mapledurham, sleepiest of places, the *Flying Dutchman* slapped the river banks with its wash and sent water into the boat of the four chosen to represent Reading Rowing Club at Henley. The crew were tired after their labours and when they had to swim for the bank one of them, possibly a victim of cramp, was drowned.

The *Daily Mail* of June 1896 reported a particularly macabre case witnessed by an old lock-keeper who was said to have seen a dozen drownings in his time (including 'a whole boatful upset by moonlight and their bodies come up one after another and float about in the lock' as he put it, almost, it seems, with a suspicion of ghoulish pleasure). He saw a young girl fall overboard and never come up again. Divers searched for her, and the lock was dragged and finally drained, all to no avail. Her body could not have been carried downstream, as the lock gates were shut. 'They said she was a beautiful young lady, too! Ah, and we sees a sight o' pretty women in the course of business!' The mystery remained unsolved for ten years, at the end of which time a valuable diamond pin was lost overboard in that same place, and the lock was again drained. The pin was found, and a reward given; also found was a circular object covered with green slime, embedded in the mud. It would not move, because it was a skull attached to a skeleton buried deep in the river bed.

Drowning cases always attracted public attention. If the victims were children or young people, lumps came the more readily to the throats of those who heard of them, if they were sweethearts the pathos was increased, and if an illicit liaison was even so much as suspected, an' added spice was given to their tragedies. The likelihood of some impropriety in the case, and the attractiveness of the lady concerned, sent people flocking to inspect the scene of a drowning fatality in Cliveden Reach in 1907. The couple involved were American—he concerned with the building of a British Columbian railway, she a very fashionably attired widow wearing a white openwork dress and blouse, silk underskirt, brown silk stockings, brown high-heeled shoes, 'a costly brown and white check cloth cloak' and a panama. 'She had a wealth of bronze hair and was a most attractive-looking, beautifully developed lady.' The cabbie who drove them from the station said that he had never seen a happier couple. Their boat struck part of a tree submerged by the water and they seem to have lost their heads and have failed to cling on. The lady's sister came down from the Russell Hotel in London to identify the body and 'when the face . . . was

uncovered she at once recognised it, and a painful scene
ensued'. The man had always spoken affectionately of his
family at home, but among his possessions, unsigned and
tantalisingly unaddressed, was found a somewhat compro-
mising letter referring to 'your charms, dearest
sweetheart . . . queen . . . your loveliness'—just sufficiently
intriguing to give a guilty thrill to the crowds who went to
gape at the spot where he was laid in Taplow churchyard with
the possible object of this passion, as they did at the spot
where they had lost their lives.

A boy of fifteen employed by a Maidenhead grocer went
swimming in the Thames with two friends one evening as
darkness approached. When halfway across the river he cried
'Help me!', and sank never to rise again. The friend nearest to
him was so alarmed that he merely struggled away, threw
himself exhausted on the bank, and burst into tears, 'while a
young man who had been bathing walked into the river as far
as he dared, and not being able to dive, stood stupefied and
bewildered watching the fast ebbing life bubbles from the
poor struggling boy beneath'. The victim died only about six
yards from the bank. At the inquest, the father 'in faltering
accents replied to the questions put by the coroner as to the
identity of the body; and then, with trembling hand, in-
scribed his name and sealed it with tears. And when the
coroner's warrant was placed in his hand, being told he could
now remove and bury the body, he seemed lost; he had, as it
were, become undertaker to his own child.'

Such tragedies were many.

> . . . never morning wears
> To evening, but some heart doth break.

25

SUICIDES, ATTEMPTED SUICIDES AND GALLANT RESCUES

A balanced account of the non-tidal Thames in its Golden Age must penetrate those yet darker shadows and bitterer tragedies which, no less than the laughter of sunshine days, play their part in its story. For the many described in the last chapter who went light-heartedly to the river intent on enjoyment, never dreaming what fate awaited them, there were others who, after weeks or perhaps months of wretched brooding despair, of turning in their minds problems beyond their power to solve, or carrying burdens of mental or physical pain beyond their power to bear, deliberately sought an end to their troubles in its gentle brown waters.

Poverty, illness or bereavement drove some to commit suicide in this way. Some had been unlucky in love and threw themselves in perhaps hoping to awaken the conscience of those who had wronged them. Others magnified small matters until they saw themselves as failures and yet others, through some mental weakness, were not answerable for their actions. Sometimes the verdict of the inquest could only be 'Found Drowned', with a pathetic list of clothing given in the newspaper report and an even more pathetic reference to the contents of pockets consisting of no money but only a handful of pawn tickets.

While criminals of all classes perpetrated huge swindles and grew fat on the wretchedness of their fellow creatures, humble men incurred tiny debts and perpetrated microscopic swindles, suffered untold anguish on account of their inability to pay and the shame to which it would expose them, and saw no solution but to take their own lives. For the sake of £3 10s a brick-moulder at the Pinkneys Green brickworks drowned himself in 1912. The money belonged to a slate club of which he was secretary, run in connection with a nearby public house, and his body was found by the vicar of Bisham floating in an upright position near the church. For the sake of about £13, a brewer's labourer, who formerly kept the Nag's Head at Marlow, and could not pay his debt to the brewers because of bad debts of which he was himself the victim, appears to have stood in the wintry river until he died of exposure. He left four or five little children. The publican of the Garibaldi at Bourne End, who had been a very quiet man, was found drowned. The slackness of business was thought to have troubled him. The body of a labourer with hands and feet tied was found in the river. His was triple misery, too heavy for endurance, for he had no regular work, had just buried a child, and he and his family were under notice to quit their home. It was thought probable that he had bound his own hands and feet.

'Things have gone very rough lately', wrote a former manager of a Leeds theatre and of an advertising company, who had been unable to work for five years and whose wife had had to take in washing and do a little charring to keep the home together. 'Things have gone very rough lately', he wrote to his son:

> . . . and I have made up my mind to put an end to it as I think I am wanted for better purposes elsewhere. I am not a bit despondent, so don't you think so; as you know I always put up a good fight wherever I am placed so that I have no fear of this or any other world . . . I feel like a slave that is just having his fetters filed off, and that I am about to start for a place where thought is free, honesty and right feeling have a chance, and I am going to another world much wider than this narrow hole of hypocrisy and misery.

There had only been a little bread in the cupboard on the last day when he had gone out to look for work, and he was found floating in the river at Windsor.

A butler who had been forced to leave his situation on account of ill health brooded on his illness and his lack of employment until he put an end to his troubles in the Thames at Windsor. An inmate of Maidenhead Union Infirmary suffering from several disabilities tried to put an end to his miserable life in the river at Taplow, but had the misfortune to be rescued. The director of a London laundry, formerly superintendent of the South India Railway Works, said to his little girl: 'Look into my eyes, you can see death there.' In India he had contracted malaria, which had left him in a weakened state with pains in head and neck which had caused him such suffering that he had once drawn a razor across his throat. One morning, having appeared even more depressed than usual, he left home to go to the office, and his family saw him no more until his body was retrieved from the Thames near Monkey Island.

The tragedy of bereavement affected a young footman employed at Hurley. Normally a high-spirited youth who cycled madly, showing off, he was very upset by the death of a brother who had drowned himself, and missed hearing from him. He too put an end to himself in the same way, leaving black-edged letters explaining that he did not feel life worth living and would be better if he was gone. He dressed himself in his bathing costume, so that his clothes could be left to his relations, and carefully corded his box and sealed it with sealing wax.

Another body, the *Maidenhead Advertiser* informed its readers in 1898, was 'comfortable' at the Hind's Head at Bray. This fortunate corpse was the property of a retired stationer, whose wife had left him, who loved children and spent most of his time with them, but had none of his own. He showed magic lantern slides at children's parties and was very fond of the little daughter of the publican at the Stag and Hounds at Braywick whom he allowed to ride on his tricycle. 'Will you attend my funeral?' he had asked her. 'Will you miss me when I die?' He was seen by the family of E. Morris, the Bray lock-keeper, walking along the towing path in heavy snow which aroused their suspicions, and later Morris noticed a hat floating down the river.

A boy who worked for a Maidenhead baker and caterer stole from his employer a cake and a few oddments which he could have bought for half-price, and this trivial matter so preyed on his mind that he went home and wrote to his brother and his sweetheart, his 'darling Nell', telling them that his body would be found in the river, and hoping that his brother would forgive him for bringing this stain upon him. He said he did not know how he could face the men at work. His cap was found at Bray weir, but his body was not seen until over three weeks later, when it was found floating downstream, having perhaps been washed up by a tug.

The suicide the most dreadful to the imagination of all those which took place in these years occurred at Hurley Roller Flour Mills in 1893. A young man of 22, described as abstemious and very cheerful in a quiet way, who was a partner in the firm, had been paying his addresses to a young lady in the village. He wrote to his father of marriage, to which came a reply in rather discouraging terms, suggesting postponement as he had not been in partnership long, and the girl was so young. Putting down a book he was reading, the young man went to his office, transacted some business and wrote to his father: 'Your letter of the 16th inst. caused me to commit this awful deed. Really I cannot live in your mistrust any longer.' He then tied a 56lb weight round his neck and jumped into the mill stream.

At Windsor a young woman wearing a black silk dress and velveteen jacket with gold watch and chain and ear-rings was seen making for the water with her hands raised, crying 'William!' and asking God to help her. She was the barmaid from the Castle Hotel, and William was the landlord's brother with whom she had 'been on terms of improper intimacy'. She had told the landlord that William had promised to marry her, to which he had replied that she was not to think of such a thing.

A great sensation was caused at Bray in 1896 when an American lady threw herself into the river after vain attempts to get her fiancé to the altar. When rescued she cried 'Leave me alone; I want to die; I am mad!', and upon the appearance of a policeman to arrest her she exclaimed to her recalcitrant fiancé, a Royal Naval engineer: 'See the result of your work! Won't you come with me?', but he refused, saying the law must take its course. In court an intrigued crowd admired her fashionable clothes and tried to peer through the thickish blue veil partly hiding her face. They applauded when, after she had promised not to attempt to take her life again, her case was dismissed, and she departed to cheers while the reluctant bridegroom, who was said to have brought her over to England and left her without friends and money, received a hostile demonstration. Later he was burned in effigy, and given 'rough music' in the form of the 'Dead March' and 'The Girl I Left Behind Me'.

Dutch courage sometimes led to suicide attempts, some comic, some tragic. A drunk leapt off Marlow bridge saying he was tired of the world, and in the Thames at Windsor (seemingly a popular place for suicides) was found the body of a man who alternated between a state of abstinence and a state of drunkenness, and had been in the latter condition for the previous three weeks. A young girl of 17 seems to have been in a similar state when she tried to throw herself from Maidenhead bridge, screaming at a passing cabbie who managed to catch her by the leg: 'Let me die! Let me die! No one wants me. I would be better out of the way.'

An old man walked into the Thames at Marlow to drown himself, cried out when he got stuck in the mud, was rescued and taken home. 'Don't be a fool, missus; look after your baby', said Reuben, a lodger at the Crown at Maidenhead, to a fellow lodger who, sitting on some empty boxes at the bottom of the garden watching him feed the fowls, exclaimed: 'Reuben, I'm —— well going to drown myself.' She had been drinking and quarrelling with her husband. Reuben's advice was ignored, for she hurried to the river and threw herself in, protested strongly when dragged up with a boathook, and tried to get into the water again.

The pathetic catalogue of suicides during this period, to which many other equally tragic cases could be added, is to some extent offset by the great heroism shown on the Upper Thames by those who saved the lives of others often at the risk of their own. 'I shall always be pleased to do my duty', said a Maidenhead chemist's assistant who received the Royal Humane Society's certificate on vellum in recognition of a very gallant rescue, and this extremely modest, almost matter-of-fact statement best typifies the attitude of the many brave men who took it for granted that the safety of others must be placed before their own. This same inbred courage took the 1914 generation of these men to the recruiting offices, and enabled them to face the prolonged misery of trench warfare and the battlefields of the Western front, of Gallipoli, Palestine and Mesopotamia.

Lock-keepers seem to have looked on life-saving as part of their day's, or sometimes their night's, work. The Teddington keeper received an award from the Thames Conservancy for making a rescue on a dark winter's night. Thacker reported that W. H. Marsh of Chertsey had made some very gallant rescues and 'the Conservancy, perhaps with a touch of official humour, insured his life'. The Penton Hook keeper (formerly at Teddington, where his son had been drowned) received a medal and certificate for jumping in to save a boy who was being carried towards the weir; and J. H. Kemp of Boveney made his seventeenth rescue in 1911.

Morris of Bray lock and his family showed great bravery and presence of mind when a serious boating accident took place in the spring of 1886. A randan had been hired by three athletic young men and 'three of the bonniest girls' the boat's proprietor had ever seen; nearly all were total abstainers, expert swimmers and well used to boating. But the river was high owing to recent rains, and at Bray the randan was forced into the weir stream, which was fierce and rapid, and three of them were thrown into the water, where they supported themselves on the keel of the upturned boat until it was dashed against the side of the weir, while the others managed to cling to a post, but only one retained his hold. One young lady, after being washed away, was able to seize a chain attached to a dredging barge, upon which Morris plunged in with a hitcher and, supporting himself on a floating pile, eventually managed to hook her by the shoulder and move her near enough to the bank for his daughter and the assistant lock-keeper to drag her on to land. His daughter, who was 17, acted 'like a little heroine'. Morris, still struggling in the water, burst into tears because he could not save one of the other girls who was grasping at a chain near to him but was forced to relinquish her hold. Meanwhile his son had put out in a dinghy in a vain attempt to rescue other members of the party. A visitor from London set out in an old punt with one scull damaged and saved the young man still clinging to the post, at the risk of his own life. Afterwards he was unable to say how he rescued him or got him to the bank. There were three victims of this accident, which was the subject of correspondence in the daily press. Morris received the Royal Humane Society's bronze medal, his daughter a vellum and his son a parchment testimonial. The *Maidenhead Advertiser* got up a subscription for Morris and he was not forgotten by the families and numerous friends of the victims of the accident, while the local superintendent of police received a 'handsome silver-mounted Malacca cane' from the family of one of the drowned girls.

A letter to the *Maidenhead Advertiser* in 1885 suggested that people scarcely recognised what they owed to lock-keepers. It praised Turner's recent action in rescuing a couple whose Canadian canoe had got too near the wash from the sluices of Boulters' gates and overturned. Only his promptitude saved them. Turner was famous for his bravery, and it was during this sixth rescue at his lock that, as already mentioned, he hurt his arm so badly that it was for some time useless.

On one occasion a boat entered Boulters containing a father with his two young children and a dog. Turner advised him to steady the boat by a chain, but this advice was ignored and, as the lock filled, the boat was forced onto a gate where one end became jammed by the sluices while the other rose, flinging the party into the water. The assistant lock-keeper threw life-saving apparatus which saved the father and his little daughter, and Turner jumped in as the son was drowning and managed to get him to land. *Baily's Magazine* commented:

> Bad watermanship and carelessness are responsible for most casualties on the river . . . at every lock may be spotted oarsmen (?) fancifully, if not faultlessly attired, with a screaming nothing-in-particular blazer, and meaningless though staring cap, who are doing exactly the wrong thing . . . They are perfectly complacent and equally inefficient, and would resent a word of excellent advice if offered.

A medal and certificate were presented to Turner at a meeting at the Ray Mead Hotel. He entered the room to the sound of prolonged applause which was renewed when he was given his certificate, framed in oak. 'After a short pause, Turner, who was much affected, replied in suitable terms.' The evening continued with the drinking of toasts and the singing of 'some capital songs', ending with 'Auld Lang Syne' and the National Anthem. The following week's *Maidenhead Advertiser* foresaw the time when Turner might possess 'enough certificates to paper a small apartment and more medals than his broad chest will properly display'.

Both A. Hill of Cookham and his brother were presented with Royal Humane Society certificates, and H. J. Tame, the keeper at Marsh lock, had by 1909 saved no less than twenty-five lives, for which he had received medals and a framed illuminated address. At Iffley lock one dark winter's night the lock-keeper's son was woken by shouts and plunged into the river without hesitation; his father had already done so, and they both received awards from the Thames Conservancy.

H. Husted, the Windsor bridge toll-gate keeper, saved several lives, and in 1901 W. Joel, Mr Grenfell's waterman, saved his nineteenth life. Sometimes in severe winter weather when people skated on the frozen river, ice collapsed under them, and they were gallantly rescued after a sobering interval in the chill water. During the great flood of 1894, Ned Andrews performed a dangerous and heroic act at Maidenhead, paddling his punt across the river which was flowing at 11 or 12mph to save the lives of three men.

Mr E. Townsend, of the boat-building firm, was awoken one foggy November night, hurriedly put on a few clothes, and punted towards the cries of the Bourne End ferryman who had fallen into the river and was being swept away. He was by then numb and exhausted and heavy in his wet clothes, but Mr Townsend, by dint of great exertions, managed to rescue him single-handed. A perhaps even more heroic action was performed by a young girl of eighteen who, fully clothed in the flowing feminine attire of 1895, jumped into the Cookham mill stream and swam to the rescue of a lady whom her courageous efforts saved from drowning.

Sometimes the reward was scarcely worthy of the deed. A Maidenhead fisherman who, in helping to raise and revive an apparently dead bather who had sunk to the bottom of the river, broke his rod and lost some of his tackle, received the generous reward of 5s; but a Marlow doctor was perhaps even less fortunate for, while he was plunging in to rescue a boy who was in difficulties after his canoe had capsized, 'some unfeeling wretch marched off with his headgear with the result that our popular medico had to borrow another man's hat'.

26

LOCK-KEEPERS

The *Maidenhead Advertiser* of 1884 described Turner's work thus:

> . . . during the eighteen or twenty hours of a broiling summer's day the lock-keeper is continuously opening and closing sluices, and guiding and directing erratic steersmen and impulsive oarsmen, and we begin to perceive that there are modern labours almost as monotonous as those of Sisyphus, and as responsible as those of Hercules. The life of a lock-keeper is one which should inspire almost as much admiration as sympathy. During the whole of the fervent summer-tide he is at the beck and call of everyone who can use a scull or twist a punt-pole, and many who have not even an elementary knowledge of oarsmanship. He has to close this gate and open that; he has to collect tolls and keep registers. He has to advise and admonish, assist or control all who come within the fifty feet or so which represent the area of his jurisdiction. And they come at all hours and in all moods and in every aspect. They come in twos and they come in twenties. Every order of mankind is represented, in singles or in groups—the man of rank, the man of wealth, the man of mind, the man of fashion, the man of folly. He is chaffed, he is lectured, he is rated, he is argued with. He has to be civil, forebearing, active, resolute, and resourceful . . . in summer he has no rest; in winter he has too much.

The Thames Conservancy's custom was to employ retired petty officers to take charge of their locks—men with the observant eye, the presence of mind, the experience, character and courage nurtured by naval service and so necessary to the manifold responsibilities of a lock-keeper's life. Their naval pensions, supplemented by rent-free accommodation, a salary (about 1890) of £30 or £40 per annum, and the money they made by the sale of flowers and vegetables and by boat-minding, gave them, in the opinion of the *Standard*, a sufficiently comfortable income, although in 1895 they were asking for a salary increase. Most of them performed police

functions as water bailiffs, constantly patrolling the towing
path, and were officers of the Thames Angling Preservation
Society. The locks from Teddington to Oxford were virtually
police centres for the river.

The lock-keeper's accounts were inspected each week, and
on busy days it was a difficult task to make a way through the
throngs of lock-loungers to collect the tolls of which an
accurate account had to be kept. ('What does that man eat
money for?' asked a small girl seeing Turner with a coin in his
mouth, and then, in a tone of disappointment when he
transferred it to his pocket: 'Oh, he didn't eat it. What a pity!')
In addition to this duty, he had constantly to watch the height
of the water and control the boats in his lock and its vicinity.
Turner had a number of assistants at busy times, and the
invaluable help of his wife who had her work cut out to book
the names of launches and the times they went through.
Lock-keepers were regarded as universal providers, and
people worried the Turners without compunction, sometimes late at night, asking for soap, a spare candle, a drop of
lamp oil, a box of matches, a can of hot water, the loan of a
boathook or punt-pole, or help in stopping a leak in a boat.

Many lock-keepers were characters; all had their stories,
some comic, some sad. Just as the river imposed a pattern on
all locks, yet each was different in its details and setting; so
their keepers, on whom their work imposed an outward
sameness, brought a different personality to each. T. Gray of
Marlow, tall, whiskery and weather-beaten, was an ex-
soldier, bringing to his waterside home beneath the Quarry
Woods a background of the parade ground and the frontiers
of Empire. Turner and the Mapledurham keeper had served
before the mast together, and had felt the bounding of the
Marlborough, a three-decked man-o'-war, beneath her full-
bellied sails. Thacker recalled Big Tom Weal, at Rushey lock
upon the stripling Thames:

> Many a talk I have had with him on his white-railed bank in the
> cool of the evening, watching Bampton spire pierce the lemon
> clearness above the trees; while Buckland woods darkened into
> ever deeper purple. The extortions of some of the River Inns,
> local drownings. his eeltraps, the winter floods, the former crazy

lockhouse and weir, his own little commerce in rushes and produce: on these he will talk by the hour with many a bit of humour his impeded speech does nothing to diminish.

By 1906 three generations of the same family had served the Thames Conservancy at Eynsham weir, above Oxford. This was a tragic family, for the old keeper's wife had been in the lunatic asylum at Moulsford for the previous eleven years, and their son joined her there after an accident to his head. To Thacker, a sympathetic listener: 'The old man recited the rustic tragedy as a bare matter of fact, seeming scarcely to question or complain. "Miss 'un more 'n the missus" he remarked, in his slow emotionless voice.' Later he had the happiness of seeing his son restored to him.

Mrs E. T. Cook, in *The Upper River* published in 1904, described shooting Hart's weir, her boat guided with a long hook by the keeper, a 'burly and genial fellow, strong as Hercules'. This exhilarating method, described also by Thacker, made the sober progress of boats through a pound lock appear a tame thing. The Hart family, who gave their name to Hart's Lock Wood, were among those families and individuals notable for long service. W. Sheppard, who retired from Mapledurham lock in 1882, first went there in the late 1820s, nearly thirty years before the Thames Conservancy came into existence. He is said to have 'skinned' the river remorselessly in the days before the size of fishing net meshes was controlled, sending as much as half a ton of small fry at a time to Leadenhall Market, but this report may be exaggerated.

James and Tom Sadler, father and son, reigned at Sonning from 1845 to 1911. James Sadler, who was in charge for forty of these years, was a great character, and if his verses did not achieve the most exalted heights of poetic fancy, his very ornamental Berkshire beehives were in large demand throughout the Midlands. His son, too, was a beekeeper, and Sonning lock was a famous place for roses. The floral tradition was continued by E. E. Light, Tom Sadler's successor, and in his day the lock often won the garden prize instituted in the late nineteenth century.

J. Thomas, at Shiplake in 1877, was a man-o'-war's man.
His successor, J. Constantine—short, sturdy and grizzled—
who served there for thirty years, was also an ex-navy man,
and flew his flag from the flagstaff on suitable occasions. J.
Scott, at Hurley from the late 1880s to 1909 after naval service
going back to the days of the old wooden ships, injured his leg
at the lock, and it had to be amputated. J. Coster, keeper at
Marlow for forty years before Gray, retired in 1886, when a
testimonial was got up for him in the district in recognition of
his 'uniform civility'. Hill of Cookham, who retired in 1914,
was described by the *Express* as one who knew his business
and was a master of both tact and sarcasm, equally adept at
holding up a launch of noisy trippers, ridiculing a 'mug'
punter with irony, and sympathetically helping ladies in-
experienced in the skills of boating.

Boating could be something of an ordeal for the sensitive
novice trapped within a lock's shiny walls, grinned at by a
mass of critical faces as he awkwardly tried to obey the lock-
keeper's only-too-pointed instructions. Gray of Marlow was
notorious for his rudeness (especially on those very rare
occasions when he chanced to notice a man on the river with
his shirt-sleeves rolled up), and Bickerdyke complained that
some lock-keepers treated river-users more or less con-
temptuously, assuming the air of policemen. In earlier years
there had been a number of reprimands and dismissals for
incivility, but Thacker expressed surprise at this, saying that
in about twenty-five years' experience of the river he had met
with only one uncivil word. Possibly, he wrote, lock-keepers:

> . . . are now of a better class than formerly: possibly also the self-
> esteem of some of the older navigators was a little too pro-
> nounced. A pleasant word of recognition, the passing of the time
> of day, will always bring you a welcoming smile and a helping
> hand next time you are through.

Hill had been Captain of the Boats at Eton, and was at
Cookham for twenty-two years before ill health forced his
retirement. A total of £140 10s was collected for his testimonial and presented by Colonel Ricardo, then High Sheriff
for the county of Berkshire. A character sketch of Thomas

Chainey, an earlier keeper at Cookham, appeared in the *Lock to Lock Times* in 1888:

> Turner's neighbour is in every respect a contrast to him with the exception that he is a very good fellow. Thomas Chainey is also a navy man . . . and like most old sailors can turn his hand to anything. In appearance he is broad built and strong; his beard is full and inclining to red, and his voice—like most sailors— distinctly audible . . . Among the numerous distinguishing features at Cookham Lock is its diminutive garden, which is its proprietor's greatest delight. His spring flowers, his summer roses, and later on, his giant sunflowers, are famous among boating folk, and happy is the fair damsel in whose honour a bloom is cut. There is, however, still one point about Chainey which remains to be told. He can tell a good story well. You have only to draw him out, and—there you are.

One Cookham lock-keeper received help from an un-expected source. At night-time his cat assumed the duties of deputy keeper. She sat near the lock gates listening, and if she heard a boat approaching scrambled up a tree by his bedroom, ran along a branch, jumped in through his open window and proceeded to comb his hair with her claws until, awakened in this curious fashion, he staggered downstairs sleepy-eyed to pass the boat through.

Other four-legged characters were to be found at locks. Apart from Turner's 'wondrous bull-terrier' Juggins, there was Skipper, a white, smooth-haired dog with black ears from which black markings extended around each eye, a creature who put duty before pleasure. According to the *Lock to Lock Times* he felt keenly the weight of his responsibility which was to keep the name of the magazine always before the public eye by means of an advertisement on a banner which he wore across his chest.

Nipper, a fox terrier belonging to the Bray ferryman, worked even harder, and all for pleasure. He was trained to the task of 'ferrying' the punt across the river. He would seize the end of a heavy rope thrown into the water from its bow and set off across stream, defying the strength of the current, and drawing up to five people at a time. When the journey came to an end he was reluctant to give up the rope, and he would also tow skiffs and dinghies.

The Morris family of Bray lock gave the Thames a lady punting champion. J. Croft, who was at Boveney in the 1880s and 1890s, was once fined for selling home-made wine without a licence. Thacker remembered him as a burly old man who 'had been a navy bo'sun and sold you little shilling autobiographies at sixpence apiece'. W. Franks of Romney, sturdy and taciturn, was 'an authority on the rainfall even to two places of decimals'. His brother was at Bell Weir lock. Formerly they had both assisted Turner at Boulters. S. Myhill, 'handsome old Myhill' as Thacker called him, once at Hambledon, was at Penton Hook from about 1907. Thacker wrote:

> I thought he looked more than ever saturnine, having added to his natural air of admiralty a still profounder aspect of austerity . . . He seemed even cosier here than there, surrounded with white crooning doves and little lawns and orchard: Myhill; with whom royalty, they say, would once step ashore and converse.

Occasionally, especially in earlier years, lock-keepers were women; perhaps widows whose husbands had kept their locks before them. About 1877 it was said of two or three of these that 'they did not open their paddles because it would wet their boots to do so'. But there was generally masculine help at hand, in the form of either a son or an assistant. Pearson's *Gossipy Guide to the Thames from Source to Sea* informed readers that excellent teas were supplied for 9d at most lock houses. Some, such as Days, offered rooms to let; milk and firewood could also be bought at Days. Keepers could arrange for campers to erect tents on their islands away from the fear of irate farmers, bulls and dogs. Mrs Hill's teas at Cookham were 1s in 1901, but could be partaken of 'on the nice shaded and secluded lawn running alongside the lock. Mrs Hill knows how to make a good cup of tea', the *Maidenhead Advertiser* noted:

> . . . and it is served up with a plentiful supply of bread and butter (nicely cut) and cake and two kinds of jam, in tip-top style. There is no stint, and into the bargain one has the pleasure of being waited upon by a nice-looking, courteous and business-like waitress.

The burlesque entertainment which featured in the *Lock to Lock Times* of Christmas 1888 included a chorus of lock-keepers (led by Turner, 'The Lord Mayor of Boulters', illustrated kicking up his heels in a ballet skirt), complaining of the constant cry of 'Lock, lock, lock!', of their irregular hours, and of the river being so much busier than it had formerly been. Reports of long hours worked at Cookham and Bray locks, especially during Henley week or Ascot Sunday, are legion. On one occasion, Morris of Bray worked all night for two nights. Turner worked over a hundred hours in several weeks of one season. He was up all one Saturday night, during the course of which he had to see to a launch with its propellor entangled in weeds in Cliveden Reach. Once he had no rest for three nights; another Saturday, after working till midnight, he had to turn out between 2am and 3am to let through a couple of electric launches whose occupants, some of whom were said to be people of title, 'were better humoured than our friend Turner, who, although a lover of vocal music, scarcely appreciated "Hi-ti" and "Ta-ra-ra-boom-de-aye" at three in the morning'. He was on duty again at 6am. On various occasions, he passed ten nights without going to bed; scarcely had time for half a meal; went to bed at 2am and was called up again to let a launch through at 2.30; and was called up at 11pm after a hard day's work by someone wanting a box of matches. By 1904 a new fashion had come in for taking supper in a boat and returning by moonlight, perhaps passing through a lock at 2am. Poor lock-keepers!

In 1903, the year of the summer floods, Turner had his first Sunday off in the season for twenty-three years, but the following October he was reported to have been so busy at his lock that he had not been into the town since Christmas. Nor could the lock-keeper's vigilance be relaxed in winter-time, for the lock, the weir, the weir-tackle, the sluices, the level of the water, all needed his attention.

Turner's garden generally won the lock-gardens' prize for its section of the river, and was described as the prettiest on the Upper Thames. In spring it was full of tulips and other spring flowers, later replaced by 'a wealth of choice begonias', roses, pinks, honeysuckle and carnations. In 1901 the roses bore thousands of blooms of varied shades, some 'of prodigious dimensions'. At either end of the garden he had placed 'a handsome marble vase, beautifully carved'. This part of the lock property was strictly private; Juggins the bull terrier too would, the *Maidenhead Advertiser* observed, resent intrusion there.

Turner retired in 1905. A letter from the mayor of Maidenhead asked for subscriptions to his testimonial to be sent to *The Times* and other dailies, and Turner decided to take this testimonial in the form of a purse of gold, which was presented to him with an illuminated address by Mr Grenfell at the annual Maidenhead Rowing Club dinner held at the Town Hall. Mrs Turner had died suddenly not long before, and Turner made an emotional reference to her in his speech, describing how many times at 4 or 5 o'clock in the morning she had stood on the bank holding a light to guide him while he had crossed in a boat to attend to the weir and regulate the water. 'God had seen fit to take her away and he was left by himself.'

Turner continued to work on the river after his retirement, when Sir Roger Palmer engaged him as his Thames bailiff. Some years later the Prince of Wales, the future Edward VIII, visited an undergraduate who was staying with the old lock-keeper, whom he was delighted to meet and with whom he had a long conversation about Boulters and the river. Turner's health failed in 1914, but he was about in his garden as usual one day in June of that year. In the evening, as if fate acknowledged it to be impossible that Turner, 'the great, imperturbable, unquestionable Turner of Boulters', should outlive the age, then within two months of its close, which he symbolised and to which he so indubitably belonged, he was suddenly taken ill and died within a few minutes from heart failure.

27

DESECRATION OF THE SABBATH:
'THE *DAY OF REST*, FORSOOTH!'

The *Maidenhead Advertiser*, having described a Sunday on
which Turner worked seventeen hours and got a snack lunch
at 3.45pm, and perspiration poured off the trolley men as they
pushed their cumbersome laden trucks up the sloping shingle
path which bypassed Boulters, was moved to exclaim:
' . . . and this was the *Day of Rest*, forsooth!'

The voice of the Sabbatarian was heard from time to time
during the Golden Age of the Thames. As the river became an
ever more popular pleasure resort and crowds flocked to it of a
Sunday in ever increasing numbers, so his sighs became ever
profounder and his head-shakings more solemn and
lugubrious. Maidenhead, where the troops of Mammon, not
to say of Satan, chiefly swarmed, was the main recipient of
these melancholy broadsides, to which the reply of that
spirited town aglow with prosperity and popularity was best
summed up in the words: 'Dost thou think, because thou art
virtuous, there shall be no more cakes and ale? Yes, by Saint
Anne, and ginger shall be hot i' the mouth too.'

Various motives and arguments moved or were used by
those who deplored the 'heathen carnival' which took place
on Sundays at Boulters and other popular river resorts.
Sincere religious feelings mingled with the killjoy Puri-
tanism, so deeply engrained in the English character over
many centuries, which regarded with horror anything akin to
the carefree continental Sunday. A desire for respectability
played its part, and a desire to rest and be quiet and permit
others to do so. A letter to the *Maidenhead Advertiser*
suggested 'that no man, prince or peasant, has any right to
cause others to work on the rest-day, merely to minister to
pleasure . . . ' The argument of the Sabbatarian was even used
in 1877 to counter an application to transfer the licence for an

inn in Maidenhead High Street to a much larger building newly erected on the river bank. The magistrates heard Maidenhead river described as 'that Pandemonium' where one Sunday not long before 300 boats had passed through Boulters, to the shame of the town! If the application were granted, they were assured that 'a greater quantity of strong drink would be poured down the throats of the Londoners visiting the river-side, and they would be more than ever in danger of drowning, and of being food for the jack'. The speaker made haste to add that he had not degraded himself by witnessing in person the disgraceful Sunday river scenes, but had received lamentable accounts of them. Moved by his virtuous eloquence and perhaps, who knows, by some more substantial persuasion on the part of a hotelier who feared his own business might be affected by the success of this application, the magistrates refused to grant it.

Maidenhead's character was again blackened by the counsel defending some roughs who had assaulted a Captain Willis on his way home after a Sunday visit to that much-maligned town. The offence took place when the captain dismounted from his tricycle in the course of what can hardly have been other than a dignified journey and went to remonstrate with the defendants, who had just put a spoke in his wheel. The defence counsel implied that he had been drinking at 'poor, misguided, corrupted Maidenhead, which is a disgrace to the country on a Sunday', and then returned in the dark with neither light nor bell. The counsel's eloquence was to no avail, however, and the roughs were sentenced. But perhaps they deserved just a little sympathy, for the temptation to put a spoke in the wheel of that curious machine must, to the uncultivated mind, have been nearly irresistible.

As late as 1907, in fact as late as 1914, that repressive spirit, which looks out from innumerable pairs of stern eyes set above rat-trap mouths of Gladstonean outline in the sepia photographs of the Victorian age, was busy in condemnation. In the summer of 1907 a church paper, the *Record*, carried an article under the heading 'An English Sunday. What I saw at Maidenhead', which described in detail the various classes of offending pleasure-seekers. The writer noted in one launch:

... a party of music hall performers and their friends conspicuous among them being a singer who earns an enormous income by singing songs that any decent-minded man or woman would be ashamed to repeat. The vulgar rich were, in fact, much in evidence, fully three-quarters of the launches being occupied by persons who possessed a considerable quantity of money and wished to advertise the fact. On several of the launches, and also in some of the skiffs, were over-dressed women with fingers crowded with diamond rings. And to many of these, I fancy, the passing through Boulters lock was the most interesting part of the day, judging from the way in which they took care that their rings should be seen by the idlers looking on. Many of the men on the launches seemed to be almost as fond of show as the women who accompanied them; and as they stood, usually with a ponderous watch-chain spread across an extended fancy waistcoat, they looked the picture of vulgar self-content. One man of this type was lunching alone in the saloon when his really fine launch came into the lock, and the way he shovelled peas into his mouth with a knife offered amusement to all but the dignified flunkey who stood behind him.

For the flaunters of diamonds and the shoveller of peas it was clear that the day's sacred character had no meaning. And as the upper middle classes, immaculate both in conduct and appearance, passed before the pained gaze of the *Record*'s reporter as they took their innocent enjoyment in the fresh air, he saw that their hearts too were black within:

The upper middle classes largely predominated in the skiffs and punts, and their form of Sunday desecration was less objectionable—if there can be degrees in the violation of the Fourth Commandment—from the fact that, of course, no servants were employed on them. Among the people in the punts and skiffs were stockbrokers, barristers, actors and hundreds of young men and women who had scarcely begun their careers ... There was no singing, no zither or banjo playing—both of which were very prevalent some ten years ago—for it is now considered bad form to do either of these things. It is bad form too, to neglect to obey instantly and without question the somewhat peremptory order of the lock-keeper. None of these apparently well-conducted young people would do anything that is considered bad form; and if they could only be brought to see that it is bad form, if nothing more, to desecrate the Lord's Day, something would be accomplished. Unfortunately it will be difficult to achieve this, for it is clear that a very large proportion of the children of the upper middle classes are being brought up to look upon boating as being the proper occupation for summer Sundays. Altogether I saw some hundreds of children in skiffs . . . and it will be difficult to bring home to these young people that the pleasure in which they have indulged in company with their parents Sunday after Sunday is not only bad form, but sinful. Perhaps in years to come some of these children will reproach their parents for having led them astray.

What was the reporter's dismay to look next upon the Sabbath debauchery of the lower orders!

The only persons I saw at Boulters Lock who did not endeavour to refrain from doing anything that was bad form were the excursionists, and their behaviour was distinctly objectionable. The quiet, well-behaved, middle-class Sabbath-breakers do not like the presence afloat of the working-class excursionists, who have nothing in common with them except that they, too, are desecrating the Lord's Day. The excursion steamers are packed with men, women and children, all of whom seem to find their greatest pleasure in yelling music-hall songs at the top of their voices. The 'singing' is led by either a piano, a cornet, a fiddle, or a gramophone—sometimes by more than one of the instruments. Apparently a large quantity of drink is consumed on these steamers, and on one, as early as mid-day, I saw two men who were intoxicated and were amusing some of the other passengers by their drunken antics. On another excursion boat were two parties of men playing cards for money. Deplorable as are the scenes upon the steamers, one cannot but recognise the difficulty of attempting to improve the state of affairs, for these excursionists naturally ask if they have not as much right to enjoy themselves as the men and women in the launches, skiffs and punts. Nor can one speak to them about drinking, without their pointing to the claret and champagne bottles to be seen on the boats of the richer Sabbath-breakers and saying that if those people have their chicken and claret, why can't we have our bread and cheese and beer?

Having made himself even more unhappy by brooding on the numbers of railwaymen, boatmen, flymen and chauffeurs forced to work at Maidenhead on the Lord's Day, the *Record*'s reporter concluded with the observation:

. . . during the eight hours that I was by the riverside I neither saw nor heard anything to remind me that it was Sunday. I heard dozens of music-hall songs, but not one hymn. The names of many prominent persons were mentioned by the well-dressed people who sat on the steps of Boulters Lock, but not once did I hear the name of Jesus Christ uttered.

And after attending service at the parish church, he went sorrowing on his way.

The mayor of Maidenhead, interviewed by the *Lock to Lock Times* in 1889, described the river as a great inducement to Sabbath desecration, affecting attendance at church and chapel. 'Our Looker-On' who wrote a weekly column in the *Maidenhead Advertiser* suggested that even the trout in the river were becoming depraved because of the cigar ends and champagne bottles thrown in, and a local councillor indignantly refused to support Sunday road watering to keep down the dust at the riverside, the council agreeing that this should be done on Saturday evenings. A one-legged tramp overlooked the day's sacred character by getting very drunk on Maidenhead bridge one Sunday; it was ignored also by the crowd of three or four hundred who followed with hooting and clamour as he was wheeled off to the police station in the special barrow kept for such emergencies. On the very brink of the outbreak of war in 1914 a Liverpool vicar was preaching on 'midnight Bacchanalian Orgies' on the river at Boulters as being 'nothing short of a national scandal'. On a Sunday following Henley regatta 'the scene he had witnessed on the boats in the lock was worthy of some of the worst records of Pagan Rome'. His indignation was swallowed up in the staccato rattle of the rifle fire of Mons, as the light-hearted young men whom he so blindly criticised took their way to a Via Dolorosa terrible beyond his imagining.

Earlier, at both Marlow and Windsor, there was trouble about bands playing on Sundays. The Lord's Day Observance Society wrote to the Queen pleading with her not to continue the custom at Windsor Castle owing to the 'unfitness of ordinary and secular amusements for the holy day of weekly rest' and the unfair competition of such attractions for those 'Christian persons' endeavouring to 'instruct the young and . . . win to holiness multitudes who are ignorant of the Gospel, and who stand in sore need of instruction in the truth of God's Holy Word'. At the Compleat Angler at Marlow a compromise was reached with the Sabbatarian element who objected to secular strains sounding from the hotel's lawn, and the band was, as the *Lock to Lock Times* put it, to be 'at liberty to discourse sweet music on Sundays without being worried by those good people who ought to have died young but did not'.

Some preachers inveighed against Sunday desecration, but others adopted a sensible attitude, encouraging boating people to attend church. There was always a good attendance at Bray, where the church porch was filled with their bicycles. Open air services of a bright character were held on alternate weeks at Bourne End and Cookham. Mr J. H. Light, the vicar of Marlow, was pleased to see members of his congregation in river dress, and issued cards of service for inspection at local hotels and boathouses.

The Bell Weir lock-keeper retired in 1886. He was a man after the Sabbatarian's own heart, for he retired because his duties kept him from church.

28

FISHING

A cartoon on Sunday fishing appeared in the *Lock to Lock Times* in 1888. A long, thin, doleful minister was shown asking a boy what his father would think of his indulgence in such a reprehensible activity on the Lord's Day. 'Don't know, guvnor,' replied the boy, 'but if yer 'tickler wants ter know, yer can ask 'im drekly, 'cos e'es only gorn ter dig sum more wurms.'

The numbers of anglers increased dramatically during the Golden Age of the Thames. *The Royal River*, published in 1885, described them as having increased a hundredfold during the previous fifty years, and by 1880, 30,000 Londoners were members of angling clubs. From the less select parts of London they poured laden with impedimenta to Paddington station, to take advantage of the cheap tickets offered to angling club members. Leslie never travelled third class on the Henley line, 'as apart from the inferior accommodation, in the summer months the carriages are often filled with parties of rough London bean-feasters, and pot-hunting bank fishermen whose conversation mainly consists of vulgar chaff, and whose beer-jugs, ground-bait, and mackintoshes smell abominably'.

A. J. Church described the 'professional bank-fisher' as commonly an artisan, small shopkeeper or clerk:

> The earliest train brings him, with his stock in trade, to the riverside. He has commonly two rods, one fitted for roach-fishing, the other a lay-by, baited with gudgeon or small dace, for some wandering jack or perch. Forked sticks to raise his rods from the ground, a square basket which has carried his provisions, and is meant to carry his spoil, and a little stool on which he sits, complete his outfit. Thus he watches his trembling quill 'till the time comes for the last train . . . [then] returned to town, the bank-fisher will often go to the weekly *rendezvous* of his fishing-club. There he and his friends will compare their captures, prizes being sometimes allotted to the heaviest.

Fishing competitions held at Marlow were unpopular with the town's professional fishermen, as competitors brought their own provisions, and, having incurred no expenses except their railway fares, laid several rods along the bank (a practice which later became illegal). Up-river angling clubs preserved their own waters, restocked them at intervals, and paid water bailiffs to prevent fish being taken below the legal size and to drag ditches to return to the main stream truants washed up by high winter waters. London angling clubs took advantage of all this without payment, and only on the rarest occasions was any contribution made to the funds of their unwilling hosts.

As early as 1879 other river-users were spoiling the angler's sport, especially in the boating season. Teddington, once famous for fishing, came to lose its pre-eminence. The *Lock to Lock Times* described fishermen as 'patient souls' harried all summer long by steam launches, picnic parties, and above all the 'tow' boat. Leslie, on the other hand, regarded them with apprehension as they sat on the river bank on their small square boxes or baskets glaring resentfully at those who disturbed the fish. Nor, in his experience, was their resentment always of a silent character, for, as he described it:

> ... they are very liable to become abusive when disturbed, as they generally have heavy bets on the weight of fish they catch. They are often as great a nuisance to the punter as he is to them, as in case the side they are on is the best one for punting on account of wind or stream, it is very hard to be expected to turn out into the deep water; they fail to perceive this difficulty, and are generally lavish with slang abuse, which if you have ladies with you is by no means pleasant.

But not all anglers were rough, abusive, or even masculine. The Countess of Wilton, accompanied by a professional fisherman, caught 2cwt of barbel in two days behind Wright's mill at Marlow. A picture published in *The Thames Illustrated by Photographs* in 1886 showed two gentlemen wearing stovepipe hats standing fishing at Teddington weir. Those who could afford to hire a punt with its attendant professional fisherman (who, if not wearing the temperance badge, was

prone to entertain his captive patron with fishing gossip
imparted on gusts of beery breath) sat moored in mid-stream
between two poles which had to be placed in position very
carefully to avoid alarming the fish. Fish were far more
plentiful in mid-stream, where they swam deep enough to be
undisturbed by the river traffic. The punt would be equipped
with chairs, fishing-rods and lines, nets, a water tank, a rake
and bait. The patron pulled in the catch, while the fisherman
did the real work, always taking care not to allow his present
employer too great a success at the expense of future patrons.
Taunt often noticed as many as twenty punts moored in close
contact at the bend of the river above Twickenham; and at
Clifton Hampden the Pennells saw, in a punt almost under
the shadow of the church, three solemn men who never
stirred except when one holding his line in his left hand lifted
up a great brown jug with his right, drank long and deep, and
handed it on. The *Maidenhead Advertiser*'s reporter in the
winter of 1884 caught an occasional glimpse at Marlow of 'an
ardent follower of "Izaak" clad in a great-coat, and cap with
ear-flaps lowered stationed in mid-stream patiently awaiting
a nibble'. James Englefield ('Red Quill' of *The Field*)
described fishing from a punt near Temple lock in bitter
weather with his feet covered with straw for warmth and how,
as the short winter's day drew to a close, rime settled on
everything about him, on his eyebrows, where it half blinded
him, on his whiskers, and on all his impedimenta. And still he
fished on, his hands swollen and numb with cold, a solitary
figure in an empty, silent landscape where nothing moved but
the gliding river.

Up-river angling clubs held their own fishing competitions. In 1891, for instance, members of the Reading
Waltonian Club went in small boats to just above Mapledurham lock, where they held a peg-down competition, and
enjoyed a picnic tea. Contests took place at Bourne End and
Cookham, followed by dinners and songs (everyone rising for
the chorus of 'Soldiers of the Queen' in 1899). Once
competitors, sitting in fifteen punts, braved a rough nor'-
easter for six hours at Cookham. The Maidenhead, Cookham
and Bray Thames Angling Association held its annual

meeting on a stormy night in 1882. Members laughed at Mr Grenfell's humorous speech, and the evening was enlivened at intervals by songs sung to a piano accompaniment 'and despite the rattling of the casements and the occasional fall of mortar or chimney pots without, the harmony was complete'.

From time to time a giant fish was caught, and sent to be 'set up'. Once such specimen was a jack which broke the scales at 27½lb and was described as 'in all probability one of the prettiest and finest fish ever taken from the Thames'. A 4lb chub caught under the Sounding Arch at Maidenhead was sniffed out by a cat while awaiting the attention of a local taxidermist, as the result of which part of its tail disappeared.

The Thames Angling Preservation Society, founded in 1838, maintained rearing ponds at Sunbury for trout and other fish and two 'deeps' at Ditton, and employed water bailiffs up to Staines. They could enter boats and seize all 'unsizable, unwholesome, or unseasonable fish' and seize unlawful nets and instruments for taking fish both afloat and on shore. Higher upstream angling clubs were founded as the years went by. Marlow's angling club dating from about 1850 was the oldest of the up-river clubs. Reading's, although not founded until the late 1880s, greatly improved fishing in that district during the first five years of its existence, and in fact was said to have kept it alive there.

Night fishing and trailing from the sterns of boats and steamers—'the pernicious and Cockney system'—in due course became illegal, and in 1896 an angler was fined for using three rods and lines above Aston ferry. The Thames Conservancy instituted fence months in 1869. By 1875 the practice of netting, which used to be done nearly every day along the river bank, had been abolished. The size of the mesh of the cornucopia-shaped hoop nets used by professional fishermen was, according to Thames Conservancy regulations, to be not less than two inches, and small fry were allowed to be taken only for bait.

Sometimes there were lively scenes with poachers whom water bailiffs caught netting or 'snatching'—an unsporting practice whereby a large triangle was fastened to a line of fine gut, well weighted, and dropped into some quiet place where fish were plentiful. As soon as it touched bottom it was violently twitched up with any fish dangling from its several hooks, attached perhaps by their backs. The Boveney lock-keeper cleverly trapped poachers who were quietly trying to let themselves through his lock at night, by chaining up the gates at one end. Poachers, when challenged, showed a marked tendency to employ what was then sometimes termed 'the vulgar tongue'. On Cockmarsh in 1879, when local bailiffs of the Maidenhead, Cookham and Bray Angling Association approached men who had been shooting jack carried up by floods, 'the abuse they received was such as would not be exceeded at Billingsgate or in the purlieus of St Giles', while on another occasion a man in 'slops and corduroy' caught fish-wiring demanded of the water bailiff: 'Don't the fish belong to me as much as to you? . . . What were they sent for then?'

Poachers were not legitimate anglers' only enemies. Although by 1875 steam launches were reported to respect anglers to the extent of slackening speed when passing fishing punts, their wash still stranded spawn and small fry. Dislodged perch spawn was eaten by larger fish. Floods also caused loss of fish, sweeping fry into brooks and ditches where they perished if not retrieved. Swans were accused of feeding on spawn, but investigations showed that they ate it only incidentally when it was attached to their diet of vegetable matter. Local angling associations offered rewards for the capture of otters. By the mid 1870s H. R. Robertson complained of the 'barbarous Philistinism' which was banishing these beautiful creatures from the Thames, and pleaded that despite their well-known destructiveness the few remaining should be allowed to survive. Richard Jefferies wrote of the otter:

> He is the last and largest of the wild creatures who once roamed so freely in the forests which enclosed Londinium . . . The red deer are gone, the boar is gone, the wolf necessarily destroyed—the red deer can never again drink at the Thames in the dusk of the evening while our civilisation endures. The otter alone remains—the wildest, the most thoroughly self-supporting of all living things left—a living link going back to the days of Cassivelaunus.

But professional fishermen and others continued to be attracted by the £1 reward. In 1891 an otter was on display in a Maidenhead taxidermist's window, and a river-keeper to the Reading and District Angling Association captured his nineteenth specimen in 1896. By 1914 they were rarely seen on the river.

While the vigilance of water bailiffs checked poaching, and the taking of undersized fish for which the penalty was a £5 fine, at the same time efforts were made towards restocking reaches from Oxford to Maidenhead with fish of various kinds. It was also hoped to restore the Thames to its former glory as a salmon river. A quantity of these magnificent fish travelled to Maidenhead from Devon in a tin can with aerating cylinders, although there was no evidence that those sent from the USA in an earlier year had survived. The Thames Salmon Association placed over 500 samlets in different parts of the waters of Teddington weir in 1901. Ova were secured and ponds made in which to place them. Salmon had not been seen in Boulters weir since the mid-nineteenth century, and Mr Grenfell, in a letter to the *Field*, commented on the fact that they had disappeared with the introduction of gas lighting and asked if the discharge of gas refuse into the Thames could have been responsible.

But the river was most frequently stocked with trout. A thousand Loch Leven trout were reported to be on their way to Windsor by the Great Western Railway in 1891; Marlow (a well-known trouting centre) was kept well supplied by the local angling association; and at towns up and down the Thames, from Reading to Shepperton, literally millions were put in over the years, often with disappointing results when thrown upon the world too small to withstand their enemies. The Buckinghamshire Wye was a source of supply before it was accidentally poisoned by industrial waste.

A trout nursery in a stream running through Caversham meadows contained thousands of trout in 1879, and quantities of Californian salmon. By the following year stocks had been supplemented by fry of S. Fario and Wycombe yearlings. In the 1880s Loch Leven trout ova were laid down in a stream in a private garden at Medmenham, and a redd

made by the side of a brook at Hambledon. The intrepid Mr
Wethered, vicar of Hurley, set up a miniature hatchery in his
vicarage greenhouse. Once when angling the reverend
gentleman hooked a trout allegedly well over three feet long.
Like Jacob with the angel he wrestled with it, if not all night at
least until it broke away and escaped from his clutching arms
after the landing net had become entangled with a disengaged
triangle. The weight of outstanding trout caught appeared in
the *Maidenhead Advertiser*; the champion, a 13lb 2oz monster
captured at Pangbourne in 1896, being placed on display in a
fishmonger's window.

Eel bucks were a familiar part of the river scene, and are
known to have been situated at Tilehurst (where they
formed an obstruction in mid-stream), at Caversham bridge,
Shiplake, Magpie Ait near Culham Court downstream from
Henley, Harleyford, Maidenhead, Bray and at the head of
Black Potts Ait. Eel bucks belonging to Lord Boston of
Hedsor sealed off the main channel below Cookham (which
he had acquired when the lock-cut was made), transforming it
into a private water. Bucks were placed on a framework
known as a stage, and when not in use they remained above
the surface, facing upstream side by side like so many
racehorses waiting for the 'off'. Woven of osier rods, they
were wide at the mouth and narrower towards the end, where
a tail-like chamber sticking out at an angle formed a refuge
where the eels migrating downstream in the autumn and early
winter avoided the rush of water. The bucks were suspended
on chains and if the river was flowing strongly two men
pressing with poles might be required to sink them, but
normally their own weight was adequate to do so. As early as
the 1870s H. R. Robertson was complaining that in some
places galvanised iron was substituted for the picturesque
osiers.

By the beginning of the twentieth century few perfect sets
of bucks remained. Movable eel-traps known as grig weels
(like larger versions of crayfish baskets) could be bought at
Eton baited, weighted and stoppered for 7s 6d each. Bucks
supplemented the harvest of mills which caught eels as the
waters brought them through. On dark autumnal nights

when the wind was stirring often hundredweights could be taken at a time.

One threat which stirred London anglers to action, united them with their up-river counterparts, and sent their hands plunging into their pockets, was that posed by claims to private fishing rights on the Upper Thames. The storms created by these claims seem out of proportion to the threat posed, for riparian owners wished to establish a theoretical ownership and did not intend to prevent the public fishing their waters, if permission was asked. But anglers were indignant on two scores. Firstly, they resented the prospect of private titles being established to reaches which they and their ancestors had fished from time immemorial without let or hindrance. Secondly, they feared for the future. They foresaw the day when a title to a private fishery could become a valuable asset, with unhappy results for them, if attempts to re-establish the Thames as a salmon river were successful. Already by 1901 an enclosure had been made between Goring and Cleeve locks, and during the previous twelve months many notice boards had appeared prohibiting sport of any kind, wrongly indicating that miles of the river were private fisheries.

The question of private rights was a complicated one. The *Law Times* pointed out in 1882: 'it is clearly established law that the right of fishing in private waters is a *profit à prendre* and cannot be acquired by the general public by any amount of user'. Sir Gilbert East thought fishing rights conterminous with manors' boundaries which in many cases were fixed in Domesday Book. A Select Committee on the Thames stated that some riparian manors did carry the privilege of private fishing, and the *Lock to Lock Times* recalled that such privileges belonged to riparian owners in Elizabethan times. Rates and tithes were now payable on the river bed within their boundaries, and tax and the poor rate on the assessed value of fishing off their lands. But Bickerdyke, in his book published in 1895, said that even if a riparian owner had held a fishery for 500 years he had to perform acts of ownership by fishing, leasing or netting it, and if the public had fished without let or hindrance, his title was doubtful. Riverside proprietors, at a meeting in 1885, decided to offer to lease angling associations fishing at an annual rental which they would repay by voluntary contributions to the associations' expenses, but unfortunately only Marlow was in favour of this very sensible scheme, the adoption of which could possibly have prevented much bitterness.

Lord Otho Fitzgerald created a flurry in 1876 by forcibly expelling an angler from the towing path near Surly Hall. A few years later anglers were threatened with legal proceedings at Abingdon; and Sir Roger Palmer was bringing a case against one of the Maidenhead, Cookham and Bray Thames Angling Association's bailiffs who had thrown a net for bait in what Sir Roger claimed to be his private waters. *The World* commented that Sir Roger had charged a host at Balaclava 'whilst all the world wondered', and it would wonder still more if he charged 30,000 indignant anglers. The case broke down on a technicality, and Sir Roger not surprisingly resigned as vice-president of the angling association. Meanwhile the Thames Rights Defence Association had been formed, sprang into action with circular and handbill, and flaunted its banners in the lord mayor's procession in 1882. New bylaws proposed by the Thames Conservancy at that time included the regulation and licensing of persons as owners of private rights of fishery on the Upper Thames, but the Conservancy gave in to the protests of the angling fraternity and agreed to an amendment. Over a decade later further bylaws proposed allowing claimants to fishing rights to use, unlicensed, a smaller mesh than was then permitted, which Henley and District Angling Association declared would ruin Thames fisheries. Once again the Conservancy bowed to the objections of anglers roused to the use of wrathful expressions not commonly associated with, although not infrequently indulged in by, practitioners of the gentle art.

Several court cases over the years aroused great interest. A Mr Layard, a lawyer, was the opponent on behalf of the angling public of Mrs Annie Smith and a Mr Lewis of Maidenhead, and later of Mr J. D. Blount of Mapledurham.

The result of the Lewis case left the rights of anglers on the non-tidal Thames as vague as ever. Mr Layard announced his intention to continue fishing in the Maidenhead waters, and in due course issued a challenge to the Riparian Owners' Association saying that he intended to fish between Oxford and London without asking the secretary of the association, and was prepared if necessary to contest the question in the highest court of appeal. The Blount case, a friendly action, was again indecisive, with the result that public rights continued to depend on the permission, good nature, or carelessness of the owners of the soil of the river bed.

James Andrews, a Maidenhead fisherman who held a licence from the Thames Conservancy, was the anglers' hero of later cases. Mrs Annie Smith's agent warned him off waters she claimed as a private fishery in Bray Reach, gave orders for his tackle to be seized, and boarded his punt where he was received with such a marked lack of hospitality that he and Andrews were shortly both thrashing about in the chill November river. Andrews alleged he was left in a ballast hole from which he only extricated himself with difficulty. When the case came up before the Maidenhead magistrates, the court was inconveniently crowded, Andrews' supporters were so vocal that the counsel for the defence protested, and when the fisherman won his action for assault they cheered him lustily. Mrs Smith stopped her winter charities in Maidenhead, explaining that this was on account of heavy legal costs incurred in fighting for her rights in her pending action in the High Court. An enthusiastic meeting was held in Maidenhead Town Hall to consider the defence of public fishing rights in Bray Reach, and a letter from Mrs Smith's agent which was read offering a subscription from her so that the matter could be fought out 'in an honourable manner' was greeted with ironic cheers. Money was contributed to replace Andrews' tackle and his punt which had been smashed after being cut adrift. The mayor of Maidenhead wrote to the local paper asking for subscriptions for the Andrews defence fund, saying that this would probably be a test case for the whole of the Thames. Mrs Smith eventually won both this case and a later one in the High Court. Andrews was convicted of

trespass on her fishery and was warned that he would be sent
to prison should this happen again.

He was again in conflict some years later, this time with the
redoubtable old warrior, Sir Roger Palmer. Again funds were
subscribed for his defence, and on this occasion interest was
expressed not only by the London Anglers' Association
(which gave £20 to the fund), but by angling associations
from various parts of the country, even as far away as
Sheffield. A variation on the well-known doggerel verse
demanded:

> If man or boy the law condemns
> For taking fish from out of the Thames
> What, pray, should be that person's dish,
> Who takes the river from the fish?

However, when Sir Roger won a dredging case on a legal
point for the sake of which case it was assumed that he had a
legal right to fisheries, the Thames Fishing Defence Fund
and the London anglers, considering Andrews' chances
negligible, withdrew their support from him and, although
others gave him financial backing, he lost his case in the High
Court.

This was the last of those unhappy incidents which,
because each side stood so stubbornly on a matter of
principle, marred the tranquillity of an otherwise tranquil
pastime on the Upper Thames in later Victorian and
Edwardian times.

29

BRETHREN OF THE BRUSH

The pastoral beauty of the river scene, a cloudy mass of foliage on bank and eyot, sunlight glancing on mirror-smooth waters, autumn mists like slow smoke rising, staring cattle in riverside meadows, soft grey stone or mellowed brick of bridge or church, cottage or mansion, the grace of swans, the varied shapes of boats, the flowing draperies of ladies' gowns, piquant faces half concealed, half revealed beneath the flattering shadow of hat and parasol—all these things were recorded by the artists of the age with the draughtsman's clearness and the poet's vision.

Thames backwaters and watermills, Marlow bridge and church, Boulters lock and Bisham woods, Cookham, and many a quaint corner and thatched cottage in some up-river town or village, formed the subjects of pictures exhibited over the years at the Royal Academy or other London galleries. In fine summer weather, upstream from Marlow bridge artists sat busy at their easels, striving with firm stroke or quick delicate stippling with their brushes' tips to take the evanescent beauty of the day before its hours slid one upon one towards the red glow of sunset. The Society of River Thames Artists, of which Leslie was president, also held annual exhibitions in a floating art gallery on the upper reaches. Fred Walker, who died in 1875, painted 'The Harbour of Refuge', based on Jesus Hospital at Bray, which became one of the well-loved pictures of the Victorian Age, and his 'Marlow Ferry' epitomises the tranquil loveliness of the Upper Thames before the less attractive features of the Golden Age grew to trouble its erstwhile peaceful waters.

Walker came of an artistic family; and as a young man was apprenticed to a wood engraver. He first became known for his work in such periodicals as *Once a Week* and the *Cornhill Magazine*, and did some illustrations for Thackeray. He was the inspiration for the character Little Billee in George du Maurier's novel *Trilby*, and an anecdote related of him well illustrates his volatile temperament. He was acting as cox to two friends who were racing a randan between Cookham and Marlow bridge, in his excitement kicking and stamping so as to shake the boat. When the randan was in the lead 'in a voice weak with anguish' he implored his friends 'Wire up, you fellows; wire up! Oh, you don't know how far they're getting ahead. For Heaven's sake, pull all you know!', and when they overtook their rival 'Walker's triumph was irrepressible; his laughter was long and loud' and his friends almost expected him to tumble overboard. Afterwards he quietened, strolling on the river bank and gazing with rapture at the Bisham woods then in their high summer beauty, later lying on the turf with his chin cupped in his hands, murmuring 'Opalescent!' as he pondered on the touch of shadow and sunlight on the distant green billowing mass.

Walker was an ardent fisherman. He was remembered sitting at work in Leslie's punt moored by Monkey Island, using as a palette (for he had forgotten to take his own) a small piece of varnished wood—the punt's backboard—and stopping from time to time to cast over the nose of a large trout which he never managed to capture. He used to stay in a cottage his mother had taken at Cookham where Leslie describes him fishing for chub beneath the willows and working by fits and starts, walking down to the river at chill times of the year for a detail for his picture. Walker's own cartoon, 'The Hurley Bird', showed him at work on the river bank, his canvas propped against a boathook serving in lieu of an easel, and a small boy well muffled up in a boat marked 'F.W.', doubtless resting in an interval between sessions of modelling for the picture 'The Bathers'.

The young artist—he was only 35 years old when he died— was a popular figure at Cookham, and Leslie relates how 'it was to the cottage of an old fisherman at this place that his body was taken on the night before its interment'. 'What, not the little model!' the old man exclaimed on hearing of Walker's death. 'Not an eye was dry', wrote Leslie, 'amongst the many artistic friends who surrounded, of their own accord, his humble grave in Cookham churchyard' to which he had been carried by the villagers. Later a plaque bearing his portrait in profile was erected to his memory at the back of the church. 'Marlow Ferry' made £1,175 in 1892; sixteen years later when it came up for sale at Christie's it was sold to Agnew's for £2,835. 'The Street, Cookham' made £1,680, a considerable advance on the sum paid for it twenty years before. 'The Harbour of Refuge' had meanwhile been presented by Agnew's to the National Gallery.

Most Thames artists painted peaceful scenes where the river's spirit was the spirit of solitude—a willowy backwater perhaps, a girl in a punt and a black and white dog, one ear up, one down, with his paws hanging over the edge; or blue smoke rising from a houseboat in some remote spot, early sunbeams shimmering through wreaths of river mist—but one of the most popular pictures hung at the Royal Academy in 1897, more talked of than any other there, showed the Upper Thames in its other aspect, as fashionable, and indeed as crowded, as Piccadilly. This was E. J. Gregory's picture 'Boulters Lock—Sunday Afternoon', showing the lock full of boats, and the boats full of an elegantly dressed multitude. It contained portraits of 'local and other personages', and was highly praised by leading art critics of the day. A copy was presented to Mrs Turner. In 1905 the original, on which Gregory was rumoured to have worked for six years, was sold for 770 guineas.

Gregory was well known in the district as a resident at various times of Maidenhead, Cookham Dean and Marlow. He was president of the Royal Institute of Painters in Water Colours, and had been awarded medals at exhibitions in Paris, Munich and Brussels. In 1901 he was a member of the special committee to select pictures to be hung at the Royal Academy that year. Gregory was on the staff of the *Graphic* for many years, where his colleagues included such illustrious names in the art world as Lady Butler, Luke Fildes, Marcus Stone and Hubert von Herkomer. He was a shy man, retiring in company, but happy cycling along the quiet lanes of the Thames Valley countryside, his wheels white with summer dust, or boating on some shady backwater.

He died in 1909 and was buried in Marlow churchyard, within a few yards of the red-brick wall past which the Thames waters slide night and day without pause, on their unceasing journey. Among the mourners were George Clausen, and Percy Wild, a member of the Royal Society of British Artists—two of the many artists who made their homes amid the quiet beauty of the river scenery which found a response in the painters of that poetic age, whose delicate images so faithfully captured its special qualities. On Gregory's tombstone a palette and brushes are carved.

George Vicat Cole, whose subjects included Bisham, Marlow, and Hart's Lock Wood, showed pictures of Pangbourne and Cookham at the Royal Academy exhibition of 1886. Pangbourne was shown in sunset's afterglow, its woods blue with mists, its waters reflecting the fiery skies, while Cookham was 'seen under the effect of storm, which bends . . . the rushes of the near water, bursts over the bridge and sways the poplars in the distance'. 'It sounds grand, perhaps,' commented the *Standard*, 'but it is only picturesque. The storms of Mr Vicat Cole may, at most, be uncomfortable'—a grudging approval, it may be, but a confession of how well the artist understood the gentle character of the scenery which formed his subject.

When Cole died in 1893, 'Atlas' of *The World* recalled:

. . . those pleasant summers when I lived upon the Thames, where, at that time, he was in the thick of his work. He was a member of our little Thames Steaming Club, and I would often find him busy on board the *Blanche* at the entrance to a silent, solitary backwater, or contemplating his just-completed work through the haze of a restful pipe . . . Those were happy days, with Cole and other brethren of the brush; George Leslie in his punt, and dear, good, kind-hearted Keeley Halswelle in the *Kelpie*, and S. P. Jackson, with his Spitz dogs, in the *Ethel*. *Eheŭ fugaces!*

Luke Fildes, under a backwater's shadowy bank at Harleyford, painted 'Fair, Quiet, and Sweet Rest'; de Breanski, who lived at Cookham, exhibited one picture of Cliveden woods, and another of Henley from above, at the Royal Society of British Artists' winter exhibition in 1888; Keeley

Halswelle's pictures sold at Christie's in 1891 included 'Hurley on the Thames'; and seven artists living in the Marlow district exhibited at the Royal Academy that year. Percy Wild's 'Morning Swim' and 'A Lesson in Punting' were shown in later years. Stanley Spencer, the Cookham artist, whose early paintings show evidence of an accurate, observing and poetic eye, won a scholarship to the Slade in 1910, where two years later he received a prize for painting what was judged to be by far the best picture of the year; and while the young Stanley Spencer was beginning his career at the Slade, the aged Holman Hunt, representative of an older and very different age, was living out some of the last days of his life at Sonning.

Many artists lived along the Upper Thames. Others came there as visitors; the Royal Academy Club always, in earlier days, went to Maidenhead for its summer outing. Miss Thompson (the future Lady Butler), who was to become famous as the painter of some of the most stirring military pictures of the Victorian era, visited Marlow to make studies of the chalk formation for 'The Charge of the Light Brigade at Balaclava'. Phil May, the well-known artist whose work featured in *Punch* and the *Graphic*, spent a summer at Marlow. And Ruskin lodged at the Crown and Thistle at Abingdon, and at Clifton Hampden stood by the river wrapt in a poetic dream while the sunset dyed the waters to an ever deeper and deeper red and then faded to nothingness, and a small boy, with that insensitivity to the higher emotions of which his species is so often guilty, hurried from one side of the bridge to the other, just in time to spit on an unlucky oarsman passing underneath.

The photographs of the age, from Taunt's professional studies, reproduced as postcards—of white-aproned women at cottage doorways in quiet riverside villages, little girls in pinafores and black stockings, old men with long white beards, and carters watering sedate horses at the river's brink—to the snapshot taken by the excursionist's Kodak, all, in their clear-cut brownness, share the quality of brooding peace so evident in the artists' oils or watercolours. But the new art form which made its appearance at the end of the age made no such selective statement. The *Lock to Lock Times* suggested in 1912 that the presence of the 'cinema man' might cause trouble in some happy homes if a man were seen with 'the only girl in the world':

> I mean if Flossie's mother should happen to see you and the dear girl on the screen going through Boulters in a punt, when she'd merely gone to see her favourite Auntie for the day, there might be trouble, you know. Heavy father with boot, big brother, and so on.

30

ATTENDANT WATER NYMPHS: THE FAIR SEX ON THE RIVER

'But I see nothing of the protruding teeth, the spectacles, the enormous feet of the traditional Englishwoman', commented a French visitor in 1905. 'No,' was the reply, 'they exist only in your comic papers.' 'Very true, very true. What lovely girls! What charming summer gowns! What delightful complexions, monsieur!' Even the least impressionable of his party, it appears, was 'finally bowled over' when they met a lady punting. 'What grace, what measured strength, what rhythmic beauty!'

The fame of the English punt girl spread far, for a 1908 edition of *Travel Magazine* (published in New York) described her 'in billowy-airily-light river dress, with lovely complexion and a soft, cultivated voice, managing her punt skilfully and gracefully'. Some years before the *Lock to Lock Times* illustrated 'The Pretty Puntress' with face tantalisingly shaded and complexion protected by a large-brimmed hat, her figure's curves accentuated by the flowing lines of drapery around her tiny waist.

River girls, it seems, fell into categories. There was the elegant, decorative creature 'who inclined to mouseline [sic] de laine and foulard', the type whom Jerome K. Jerome had in mind when he described the difficulty of picnicking with girls in a natural setting where the grass was dusty and the trees, it was apparent, had not been brushed for weeks. Then there was the athletic young lady in serge and sailor hat, whose presence the *Daily News and Leader* noted on Ascot Sunday in 1912:

> ... with her pretty face and bare arms sun-kissed with freckles, like the markings on a partridge's egg. She was not the languid Ascot beauty, with her panier [sic] and her ostrich plumes, and her sweeping train of canary yellow; she was a serviceable, sturdy

water-nymph in a serviceable, simple gown, unafraid of frogs or splashes—a veritable Undine for watermanship.

There was also a solitary alarming specimen of womanhood espied at Marlow town regatta in 1884 by the *Maidenhead Advertiser*'s reporter:

> I could not refrain from a grin at the 'strong-minded' garb of one of the fair sex. Her hair was dressed as is the fashion, but instead of being covered by a hat, it was crowned by a gentleman's cricket-cap. Her bodice was a gentleman's boating-shirt, whilst the tie was similar to those worn by sportsmen, and fastened in like manner. Here, however, the masculine appearance ended, for, instead of the flannel trousers one might almost have expected to see, was a plain print skirt. Is there any need after this for a 'Dress-Reform League'?

A woman who rebelled against the enchanting fashions of the age was an oddity indeed. The contrast of male and female attire—the straight masculine, the curvaceous and flowing feminine—the public expectation of a high moral standard, and the system of chaperonage, all served to render a flirtation doubly delicious and a conquest doubly triumphant. 'Madge' of *Truth* noted at Boulters one year a pretty girl putting to best advantage the battery of charms supplied by nature and milliner. She wore 'a pink batiste frock and rose hat, tilted well forward with a cache-peigne of the palest blue ribbon. She had beguiling eyes, and made great play with them, without letting the game be too obvious. A deliberate form of making eyes is like setting the snare in sight of the bird.'

Colour schemes were chosen with care. A boatload of men and girls was noticed, the occupants 'all attired in costumes of pink and white flannels; the men with caps to match, and the girls with wide-brimmed soft straw hats turned up in folds at the back of the head, and trimmed with pink flowers and green leaves'. Near Cleeve lock in the 1880s, the author of *The Royal River* saw 'many a boatload of flannelled rowers and pink-vested sirens. Ladies', he noted, 'appear to have recognised, with intuitive taste, that pink and white are two of the most effective colours for river wear, and the Thames, in all the fashionable reaches, owes much of its vivacity to the brilliant hues of its attendant water-nymphs.' In 1893 the ladies of the Abney House eight at Bourne End were dressed in white, with ties and hatbands of Leander cerise; and at Henley one year guests arrived on board the houseboat the *Golden Grasshopper* to find their hostess wearing the boat's colours (white and yellow) and a gold grasshopper brooch.

The *Lock to Lock Times*'s fashion article featured a hair ornament in the form of a little silver scull; and in 1888 suggested the design of a dress suitable for warm weather on the river. This consisted of white muslin sprinkled over with *petit pois* in mauve with a separate and outer *veste* jacket of mauve *glacé* silk, made open down the front with small *revers*, and purple tinted pearl buttons. The same silk was to be used for the cuffs. Gloves were to be of suede kid, with *en tout cas* to match. The flat-crowned hat, one of the very newest Paris shapes, accompanying this delightful outfit was to be decorated with purple tulle, its crown encircled by silk ribbon of the same colour ending in a large bow which fastened with a tuft of mauve-tinted cornflowers. Some wore mourning for the German Emperor on the river that summer; the ladies were clad in black and white, 'and the lords of creation appeared in hats with black bands and neckties of the same sombre hue'. Again in 1910 ladies wore half-mourning for the King on Ascot Sunday and 'many of the sterner sex', too, 'fell into line with mauve shirts and neckwear'. A colour described as 'aeroplane blue' appeared, and the striking black and white costumes of some of the ladies were elaborated with marvellous displays of ostrich plumes.

'Zoélia', a perfumed extract to counterbalance the river wind, was guaranteed to keep hair in curl, and Rowland's Kalydor to guard the fair whiteness of English skins against the sun's disfiguring rays. In the late 1880s rather ugly hats with high crowns and large brims projecting over the brow were in fashion, and a member of a theatrical company was espied at Paddington en route for the river topped with cradle-shaped headgear piled high with ornament surmounted by singing birds. But the purpose of the hat was to flatter as well as to protect, and almost every one created for river

wear between the years 1870 and 1914 enhanced its wearer's
beauty. Even small straw hats, like those worn by men for
boating, were an asset to pretty feminine faces when worn
tilted at a becoming angle above simple, practical river
costumes. Most were bigger, and combined with frothy
parasols to shelter fair skins, but few parasols were seen at
Boulters on Ascot Sunday 1908, for hats had become so huge
as to perform that function unaided.

The article on fashion in a *Lock to Lock Times* of 1891
featured a nautical dress decorated with anchors on cuffs and
skirt, and described 'a big hat with a transparent brim, under
which a pretty face would look quite bewitching' which was
decorated with 'bunches of what-o'-clocks and cornflowers.
The back ... was caught up carelessly with a bunch of the same
flowers, to show the hair.' Crocodile shoes were advertised for
13s a pair, and ladies who 'coveted a high instep' were
informed that instep pads for stitching inside the tongues of
boots and shoes were 'procurable for a trifling sum'. A hat of
paille de riz with cornflowers, wheat and poppies was seen at
Maidenhead in 1888, and a high-crowned one in 'brilliant
scarlet crepe, topped with equally ruddy poppies, was a
notable point of colour amongst the many that flooded
Boulters Lock with their varied tints'. On Ascot Sunday 1906
a few hand-painted dresses were to be seen, and hats prettily
ornamented with real flowers. By the time of that festival in
1908 Dolly Varden bonnets were in fashion. Some of the
gigantic hats were trimmed with roses almost as big as
cabbages, and chains of daisies or other flowers decorated
smaller mushroom- or cone-shaped ones. The fact that some
members of the fair sex appeared at the Engineers' and
Fishermen's Regatta at Maidenhead in 1905 'exhibiting a
wealth of artistically-arranged tresses' but wearing no hats
was regarded as strange.

The World sent a reporter to Maidenhead in 1877 to
describe a Sunday at that Sabbatarian's purgatory. There he
saw two ladies on Skindles' lawn:

> ... charmingly arrayed for the present occasion, emulating as to
> colour the lilies of the field rather than Solomon in his glory.

Yonder pair of white ladies may have stepped out of one of Mr
Tissot's pictures. They are just as *blanches et blondes*, as strongly
eyebrowed and as redly lipped, as rosy of face and ethereal of
outline, as the nymphs of his imagination.

And on the very last Ascot Sunday of the Golden Age of the
Thames, red and white were the predominant colours. The
Daily Mirror described simple white dresses, 'with sweet
garden hats trimmed with pink ribbons or red berries . . . Red
sunshades, red sashes, red ribbons were to be seen everywhere.' Thus the colour that was soon to assume such a
ghastly significance adorned those fair forms, those visions of
ideal beauty whose memory the young river man was so soon
to carry with him to battles which were to leave in ruins the
world which he and they inhabited. 'Having seen all things
red,' Wilfred Owen was to write of those sacrificial victims of
that war,

> Their eyes are rid
> Of the hurt of the colour of blood for ever.

31

THE END OF AN ERA

There were many changes, many developments, both in Great Britain and her vast Empire during the four and a half decades of the Thames' Golden Age—and in these the riverside towns of the Upper Thames bore their part. But change took place within a framework, and the Englishmen who sought their relaxation on the river in those years when Queen Victoria, gazing with sinking heart on Mr Gladstone's grim visage, first received him as her Prime Minister, did not differ in kind from those who clamoured at the recruiting offices that fateful summer when Sir Edward Grey, watching the lamplighter extinguishing London's flaring pools of brightness, spoke with poetic insight of the going out of the lamps of Europe. As feminine fashion altered, yet the intriguing remoteness of the feminine ideal remained; so men, differing one from the other in minor things, responded to the same loyalties, were dreamers of the same dreams.

'We are a martial folk', wrote 'Our Looker-On' in the *Maidenhead Advertiser* in 1888; and in 1907 'War's rough game strengthens the thews, and makes the nerves of men . . . when men are no longer spurred and exhilarated by the struggle, then, indeed, has the decadence of the race set in.' At Maidenhead's parish church, at a special service to mark Queen Victoria's Diamond Jubilee in 1897, the vicar took for the subject of his sermon the Empire, ninety-three times bigger than the United Kingdom, the welfare of whose vast population was the responsibility of the British race who were 'stewards of that treasure'. In words on which time has set its ironic seal, he told his congregation: 'Our great Empire seems safe, as far as we can judge, from all human overthrow, and far from any wide-spread symptom of decay.'

As the bugles blew to battle in that hot August of 1914, and men who by descent or loyalty belonged to England re-

sponded to that call from the East Indies to the West, from
the prairies of Canada to the South African veldt, from New
Zealand's sheep-farms to Australia's outback, so along that
silvery gleam through England's heartland—that 'aqueous
dwarf' as an American described it—boats lay still and
unused in boathouses, their shining sides no longer patterned
with the reflections of sunny ripples, their oars no longer
letting fall cascades of diamond drops, fishing-rods were laid
by, the trade of riverside hotels slowed to a trickle. German
waiters and the members of German bands returned to the
Fatherland, and Englishmen of military age who had sought
their pleasure on the Thames—boathook fiends and winners
of Henley's Diamond Sculls, lock-loungers and punting
champions, 'Arries and aristocrats—all underwent a trans-
formation. The 'river knut' whom the *Daily Mirror* reported
that summer as attired in:

> . . . faultlessly creased trousers, just allowing three inches of
> white sock to be seen, white shoes and white shirt, in which there
> was the faintest suggestion of blue stripe and a soft collar and
> tie—to distinguish him from the rest of humanity . . . his
> hair . . . parted on the side and allowed to fall in a sort of plume

became a different man. Puttees replaced the faultlessly
creased trousers, his plume of hair was trimmed to military
shortness, and his immaculate white, like 'Arry's striped
blazer which was loud enough to be heard half a mile off, gave
way to the drab uniformity of khaki. Paddington which led to
the Thames and its delights was no longer to be his
terminus—rather Victoria or Waterloo, leading him to har-
bours and thence from England's shores, never, it may be, to
return.

One day after the outbreak of hostilities, the term 'the
Great War' was used by the *Maidenhead Advertiser*. The
war's full horror was foreseen, as 'a veritable Armageddon,
the consequences of which are terrible to contemplate'. The
Army Reserve and Territorials were called up, and street
musicians replaced their ragtime and other popular tunes of
the day with patriotic airs and the British and French national
anthems. The local 'G' company of the Fourth Royal

Berkshire Regiment (colloquially known as the 'Bloody Berks', pronounced 'burks') also marched to the station, where they were seen off by wildly cheering crowds, and fifty-three raw recruits marched that same way, singing 'Tipperary', 'Put Me Amongst the Girls' and 'We Are the Berkshire Boys'. All the single men employed at Cliveden enlisted; their jobs were kept open and their wages paid. Maidenhead became a military town, soon to be occupied by over 4,000 troops. Their khaki-clad figures filled the streets, the sound of the bugle rang out early and late, and the river flowed forgotten beneath the Cliveden woods.

At Taplow Court, Lord Desborough, soon to lose two of his three sons on the Western Front, directed his public spirit and boundless energies to the war effort. He offered his home for use as a hospital, and another house at Taplow which he promised to equip at his own expense. He placed his boats and watermen at the disposal of the military guard established at the Sounding Arch, was sworn in as a Special Constable, took charge of a local Volunteer Force formed to help in defence operations to relieve Territorials of local and other duties, and invited the newly formed United Arts Rifles, of which he was president, to Taplow Court for manoeuvres and general field work. Lady Desborough and two other ladies wrote to the *Maidenhead Advertiser* asking for volunteers for a working party they planned to establish at the Town Hall to make additional garments for naval and military hospitals. The Honourable Monica Grenfell, Lord and Lady Desborough's elder daughter, became a nurse at the British Hospital at Boulogne, where her brother Julian was to die of wounds.

Meanwhile, Harrison, Turner's successor at Boulters, who was on the Naval Reserve, was called up and transformed into Colour Sergeant Harrison of the Royal Marine Artillery, serving at Ostend. J. Willey of Cleeve was to become Chief Petty Officer Willey DSM; F. C. Coley of Shepperton was to receive the DCM. At Reading and Windsor barracks, as men set off for the front, the sound of their marching footsteps lessened and died away. At Maidenhead the Brigade of Guards' Boat Club was deserted. Regattas ceased. The fireworks that might have been became Very lights seen far off by soldiers' eyes, and all along the river from Trewsbury Mead to Teddington, as autumn nights closed in, leaves falling from trees which overhung the stream—poplar and willow and sycamore, oak, elder, ash and thorn—glided slowly away amid small disks of foam which danced here and there on the water's surface, and were seen no more.

ACKNOWLEDGEMENTS

I would like to thank Mr and Mrs N. Townsend of Bourne End for first introducing me to the *Lock to Lock Times*; the Thames Conservancy Division of the Thames Water Authority, and Mr T. Middleton, former editor of the *Maidenhead Advertiser*, for giving me research facilities; and Mr S. Davis and Mr J. Cowan for allowing me to study their extensive collections of old books about the Thames. I would also like to acknowledge the enthusiastic help given to me in the selection of illustrations by Mr Cowan, Mrs P. M. Curtis of Maidenhead Library, and Mr B. B. Wheals of the Bourne End Residents' Association; and to record the fact that the late Mr E. C. Cheesman eased my transport problems on several occasions.

And I would like to thank my mother for listening to it all.

Acknowledgement is due to the following for supplying illustrations: Bourne End Residents' Association (10, 11, 16, 17, 18, 19); British Railways/Oxford Publishing Company (1); Mr J. Cowan (4, 6, 7, 8, 12, 13, 15, 20, 21, 22, 23, 24, 25, 26); Maidenhead Library (2, 5, 9, 14).

BIBLIOGRAPHY

Journals

The *Lock to Lock Times* and the *Maidenhead Advertiser* were my chief sources. Also referred to are: *Badminton* magazine; *Baily's Magazine*; the *Daily Chronicle*; the *Daily Express*; the *Daily Mail*; the *Daily Mirror*; the *Daily News and Leader*; the *Daily Telegraph*; *The Dwarf*; the *Evening News*; *The Field*; *The Hawk*; the *Lancet*; the *Law Times*; the *Morning Post*; the *Paddington Times*; *Punch*; the *Record*; the *St James's Gazette*; the *Sketch*; *Sporting Life*; the *Standard*; *Travel Magazine*; *Truth*; the *West End Review*; *The World*.

Books

Armstrong, Walter, *The Thames from its Rise to the Nore* (J. S. Virtue, 1889)

Ashby-Sterry, J., *The River Rhymer* (W. J. Ham-Smith, 1913)

Bacon's Guide to the Thames from London to Oxford, 5th edition (G. W. Bacon & Co Ltd)

Belloc, Hilaire, *The Historic Thames* (J. M. Dent & Sons Ltd, 1907)

Bennet's Map and Guide to the Thames (1890)

'Bickerdyke, John' (the pen-name of C. H. Cook), *Thames Rights and Thames Wrongs—a Disclosure* (Arch. Constable & Co, 1895)

Bolland, R. G., *Victorians on the Thames* (Midas Press, 1974)

Brown, Bryan (ed), *The England of Henry Taunt, Victorian Photographer* (Routledge & Kegan Paul, 1973)

Byrne, L. S. R., and Churchill, E. L., *The Eton Book of the River with Some Account of the Thames and the Evolution of Boat-Racing* (Spottiswoode, Ballantyne & Co Ltd, 1935)

Church, Alfred J., *Isis and Thamesis: Hours on the River from Oxford to Henley* (Seeley & Co, 1886)

Compton, Piers, *Victorian Vortex* (Robert Hale, 1977)

Cook, Mrs E. T., *The Upper River* (Geo. Allen, 1904)

Cornish, C. J. (FZS), *The Naturalist on the Thames* (Seeley & Co Ltd, 1902)

Dickens' Dictionary of the Thames (1893)

Englefield, James, *The Delightful Life of Pleasure on the Thames by Red Quill of the* Field (Horace Cox, 1912)

Hall, Mr & Mrs S. C., *The Book of the Thames, From its Rise to its Fall* (J. S. Virtue & Co Ltd, 1859)

Harrison, A., *The Thames Guide Book from Lechlade to Richmond: For Boating Men, Anglers, Picnic Parties, and All Pleasure-Seekers on the River* (1890)

Higgins, Walter, *Father Thames* (Wells Gardner, Darton & Co Ltd; undated, but not after 1924)

Hutton, W. H., *By Thames and Cotswold* (Arch. Constable & Co Ltd, 1908)

Irwin, John, and Herbert, Jocelyn (eds), '*Sweete Themmes*': *A Chronicle in Prose and Verse* (Max Parrish, 1951)

Jerome, K. Jerome, *Three Men in a Boat* (Dent, 1889)

Krausse, A. S. (ed and compiler), *A Pictorial History of the River Thames* (Chatto & Windus, 1889)

Law, David, *The Thames Oxford–London* (20 etched plates) (Geo. Bell & Sons, 1882)

Leslie, George D. (RA), *Our River* (illustrated by the author) (Bradbury, Agnew & Co, 1881)

Leyland, John, *The Thames Illustrated: A Picturesque Journeying from Richmond to Oxford* (Newnes; undated, but not after 1897)

Mackay, Charles, *The Thames and its Tributaries; or Rambles Among the Rivers* (Richard Bentley, 1840)

Manning, E. D., *Delightful Thames* (rhymes, with engravings by I. D. Cooper) (Sampson Low, Marston, Searle & Rivington, 1886)

Menpes, Mortimer (RI) (illustrations), and Mitton, G. E. (text), *The Thames* (A. & C. Black, 1906)

Mosley, Nicholas, *Julian Grenfell: His Life and the Times of his Death 1888–1915* (Weidenfeld and Nicolson, 1976)

The Oarsman's Guide to the Thames & Other Rivers, by a member of the Leander Club (probably 1852)

Pask, Arthur T., *From Lock to Lock: A Playful Guide to the Thames from Teddington to Oxford* (undated, but not after 1882)

Pearson's Gossipy Guide to the Thames from Source to Sea (undated, but known to be Edwardian, probably before 1906)

Pennell, Joseph and Elizabeth, *The Stream of Pleasure* (1891)

Pound, Reginald, *The Lost Generation* (Constable, 1964)

Prowse, Keith (Launch and Boat Agency), *A Short Guide to the River Thames* (c1905)

Robertson, H. R., *Life on the Upper Thames* (Virtue, Spalding & Co, 1875)

Rowe, R. P. P., and Pitman, C. M., with contributions by others, *Rowing* (in a volume with *Punting* by P. W. Squire) (Longmans, Green & Co, 1898)

The Royal River: The Thames, from Source to Sea (Cassell & Co Ltd, 1885)

Senior, William (Red Spinner), *The Thames from Oxford to the Tower* (etchings by F. S. Walker, RHA, RPE) (John C. Nimmo, 1891)

Taunt, Henry W., *A New Map of the River Thames from Oxford to London from entirely new surveys, taken during the summer of 1871: with a guide, giving every information required by the tourist, the oarsman, and the angler* (Oxford)
—————— *A New Map of the River Thames from Thames Head to London* (undated, but probably late 1880s)
Thacker, Fred S., *General History of the Thames* (1914)
—————— *The Stripling Thames* (1909)
—————— *The Thames Highway: Locks and Weirs* (1920)
The Thames (illustrated by photographs), first series, Richmond to Cliefden (A. Marion, Son & Co, 1886)
The Thames and Its Story: from the Cotswolds to the Nore (2 vols) (Cassell & Co Ltd, 1910)
The Thames. Putney to Cricklade (illustrated guide book) (Ward Lock & Co; undated, but after 1918)
Up the River from Westminster to Oxford (with 140 illustrations and map) (Waterlow & Sons)
Vincent, J. E., *The Story of the Thames* (Smith Elder & Co Ltd, 1909)
Wack, Henry Wellington (FRGS, GP), *In Thamesland* (Putnam's Sons, The Knickerbocker Press, 1906)
Walford, Edward (MA), *Greater London—A Narrative of Its History, Its People and Its Places* (2 vols) (Cassell & Co Ltd, 1894)
Walker, J. Wesley, *A History of Maidenhead* (The St Catherine Press, 1931)
Woodgate, W. B., *Boating* (Longmans, Green & Co, 1889)

Booklets

Ford, J. W., and Smith, J. N., *Guide to Marlow* (The Marlow Printing Co, c1905)
Tomalin, G. H. J., *The Henley Royal Regatta since 1839* (a pictorial review) (Julian Berrisford Associates, 1972)

INDEX

For individual lock-keepers and regattas, see under the general heading.
Numbers in italic type relate to the plates.